Fear:
Face It

Cowards die many times before their deaths,
The valiant never taste of death but once.

Shakespeare's *Julius Caesar*

THE **mananam** SERIES

THE **mananam** SERIES

Fear:
Face It

CHINMAYA PUBLICATIONS
CHINMAYA MISSION WEST PUBLICATIONS DIVISION

Chinmaya Publications
Chinmaya Mission West Publications Division

P.O. Box 129
Piercy, CA 95587, USA

Distribution Office
560 Bridgetowne Pike
Langhorne, PA 19053
Phone: (215) 396-0390   Fax: (215) 396-9710
Toll Free: 1-888-CMW-READ (1-888-269-7323)
Internet: www.mananam.org
               www.chinmayapublications.org

Central Chinmaya Mission Trust
Sandeepany Sadhanalaya
Saki Vihar Road
Mumbai, India 400 072

Credits:
Editorial Advisor: *Swami Tejomayananda*
Consulting Editor: *Swami Shantananda*
Series Editors: *Margaret Dukes, Neena Dev, Rashmi Mehrotra*
Editorial Assistant: *Vinni Soni*
Cover Photo: *Michael Hollingshead*
Inside Photos: *David Dukes*
Production Manager: *Arun Mehrotra*

Library of Congress Control Number: 2006938158
ISBN: 978-1-880687-93-2   1-880687-93-3

Contents

FACING FEAR: STEP-BY-STEP

Preface

Many of us live in fear. We fear losing a job, not having friends, not finding a person to love, or fearing what others will think. Some of us fear small spaces, some of us fear large spaces, but the greatest fear, common to most, is the fear of dying. This fear and all other fears can be traced to that *one* fear, which is fear of the unknown. Thoughts such as: What will happen when I die? Where will I go? What will happen to my family if I lose my job? arise from the fear of not knowing the future.

Fear is a natural instinct in all beings. It is a protective mechanism that can be helpful. For instance, the fear of becoming sick can help us make better choices in caring for our health. But when we get overwhelmed with fear and, as such, it begins to control our lives then we feel the need to understand it and learn how to deal with this powerful emotion.

Only by transforming the *unknown* to the *known* can we lessen the hold of fear on us. For example, a surgeon who *knows* the technique of surgery, and who also understands its emotional and physical impact on the patient will be able to operate with full confidence. Similarly, a patient who understands the procedures and knows what to expect will be less anxious about the surgery.

In the same way, to overcome our fears we first need to understand them. The authors in this book answer questions such as: What is fear? Why do we have fear? Where does fear come from? And how do we overcome it? The insights they provide will help us lead happier lives instead of being at the mercy of the emotion of fear. In Part One, we learn how fear originates, the many forms it takes, and what happens to our body and mind when we experience fear. In Part Two, we are given practical methods to minimize the negative effect of many of our imaginary fears through prayer, breathing exercises, and visualizations. In Part Three, the authors point out that deep spiritual understanding of our true nature is the only way to become fearless.

Through understanding and facing our fears we remove much anxiety and stress from our lives. When our minds become more peaceful, we rediscover our innate love and goodness and we are able to lead fuller and happier lives.

The Editors

PART ONE

Understanding Fear

Nothing in life is to be feared,
It is only to be understood.

Marie Curie

Where there is desire, anger, and greed there will also be fear. Some people have a general feeling of fear without knowing its cause. How can these fears be removed? It can be done only by realization of the Truth and abidance in our nature as the one non-dual, Absolute Reality. The moment we create duality, a distinction between "you" and "I," there is fear. We ourselves create divisions and then become afraid of the other. But if there is recognition of the one non-dual Reality, there will be no fear.

When I know that I am this Self, and I am not this body, mind, intellect, or ego, then there is no room for grief, fear, and delusion. Brooding over the past leads to grief. Wondering what is going to happen in the future causes fear. In the present we are full of confusion. Grief, fear, and delusion will also persist as long as we remain within the framework of time, but when we gain the knowledge of the Self which is beyond the three periods of time, then they all disappear.

Swami Tejomayananda

I

About Fear

by Swami Sivananda

Fear is an instinct common to every living being. It is universal and can overpower one at any time. A king is afraid of his enemy. An academic is afraid of his opponent. A beautiful woman is afraid of old age. A lawyer is afraid of the judge and his clients. A wife is afraid of her husband. A student is afraid of the teacher. A frog is afraid of the snake. A cobra is afraid of the mongoose. No one is absolutely free from some sort of fear.

The Sanskrit equivalent for fear is *bhaya*. Fear is an emotion or *vrtti* in the mind that is produced when one's life is in danger. There are various degrees of fear; there is simple fright, timidity, shyness, alarm, and terror or extreme fear. Extreme fear is characterized by pallor of the face, palpitation of heart, slowing or stoppage of pulse, tremor of limbs, perspiration, expressionless condition of the eyes, and in extreme cases, choking of voice, inability to speak, and so on. The body becomes like a log of wood and the mind becomes stunned. The functions of the senses are inhibited and in extreme cases one may die of shock. In most cases, however, when the cause of fear is removed, one slowly recovers from the morbid symptoms and comes back to one's original state.

Fear is of two kinds; namely, normal fear and imaginary fear. The percentage of normal fear in people may be only ten, while imaginary fear accounts for the other ninety percent. Normal fear is healthy, paving the way for one's progress. It preserves life. Imaginary fear causes diseases, depletes one's energy and produces all kinds of feverish excitement, low vitality, uneasiness, discomfort and disharmony. Whenever there is an epidemic, fear is the predominant cause of death. Imagination causes serious havoc and one becomes a victim of the actual disease due to stress of fear.

Following are some examples of how imaginary fears affect people. A student prepares himself day and night for an examination. He has passed all the preliminary examinations with credit, but he develops some kind of imaginary fear — examination fear. And as soon as he enters the examination hall, he becomes nervous and confused. His hands tremble and he is unable to answer the questions and fails in the final examination. Another example: two friends meet after a long time. Somehow they talk all night about the evil spirits. These thoughts go deep into the subconscious mind of one of them and he began to dream that the room in which he slept was haunted and that an evil spirit tried to do some mischief. From that day onward he began gradually to lose his health. This was all due to imaginary fear. Some imagine and think: "What will be my fate if my husband dies? What will happen to the children and me?" Most of us have some kind of imaginary fear. There is no end to them.

Peculiar, irrational, and unnatural fears are called phobias. A phobia is an unnatural form of fear with no objective reality. There is nothing to frighten people, no threatening situation in their environment that should cause fear in them, yet they cannot free themselves from this emotion and its attendant negative feelings. Phobias are also endless. The causes of phobias are nervousness and lack of correct thinking and clear understanding.

The origin of the most neurotic fear can be traced to childhood. The seeds of fear may lie dormant in childhood in the subconscious mind. They sprout forth during periods of crisis or stress. The minds of children are very impressionable. Mothers and friends should be very careful when they deal with them and should not tell the children anything that may frighten them. Instead, they should tell stories of chivalrous deeds that will make their children bold and courageous. During pregnancy, mothers-to-be should read inspiring books like the *Rāmāyaṇa* and the *Śrīmad Bhāgavatam* if they wish to bring forth intelligent and brave children. Parents and teachers should have elementary knowledge of child psychology; then alone can they mold their children properly.

Causes of Fear

The cause of fear is ignorance. When we forget our original, divine nature, we get caught up in the whirlpool of ignorance. The infinite fearless *Brahman* became the finite *jīva* with fear. Identification of the body or *dehādhyāsa* is another form of ignorance. This physical body is an instrument for sensual enjoyment and when we suffer from any disease, we are afraid that we will lose our body, which serves as a vehicle for our enjoyment. We try our very best to preserve this body. All other causes of fear are traceable to body identification.

A feeling of inferiority is another cause of fear. This negative feeling produces lack of self-reliance or self-confidence. One is afraid of those who have superior talents, power, position, and efficiency, which makes one feel that he/she is incapable of doing anything. Some physical deformity or deficiency, lack of physical and mental efficiency, and wrong training in children are other causes of fear.

Fear in all its different aspects is the greatest enemy of man. Constant fear saps the vitality and destroys one's ability and confidence, which makes one powerless. It is a great enemy of success. What paralysis does to the physical body, fear does to the mind. It is a most destructive emotion. It breaks down the nervous system and undermines health. It creates worry and renders happiness and peace of mind practically impossible. Clinging to life and body, or love of earthly life, are the main causes of all fear.

Fear is Illusory

Fear is illusory; it cannot live. Courage is eternal; it will not die. Perils, calamities, and dangers are the certain lot of every person who is a citizen of this world. Therefore, fortify your mind with courage and patience. Fortitude, courage, and presence of mind will sustain you through all dangers. Just as a rock on the sea-shore stands firm against the dashing waves, even so a person who is endowed with courage is not affected by the dark perilous waves of this endless cycle of births and deaths (*saṁsāra*).

A courageous person does not tremble in the hour of danger. He stands adamant in challenging conditions and circumstances and comes out victorious. He is not embarrassed and bewildered. He does not sink down. He is not overwhelmed by despair. He smiles away all dangers and difficulties and blowing the trumpet of triumph attains victory in the end.

The threatening of fear is a terror to the heart. Lead a virtuous life. Live in God. Be good. Serve. Love. Give. Meditate. Then nothing can frighten you and the Lord of Death will be afraid of you. The terrors, even of death, will be no terror to you.

Do not terrify your soul with vain imaginary fears. From fear proceeds misfortune and failure. The fears of a coward expose him to danger. A coward dies many times before his actual death. Be bold. Be cheerful. Allow not your heart to sink from the fantasy of imaginary fears. Have self-confidence and faith. Your birthright is courage. You are a child of light. You are an offspring of Immortal *Brahman*. Claim thy Birthright now. Rise Up! Roar OM! OM! OM!

II

Sources of Fear
by Swami Tejomayananda

What are we afraid of in life? Primarily we are afraid of losing something, we are afraid of losing our job, our health, family or friends, or our name and fame. This is the single common factor in any situation of fear, the fear of losing something. Sometimes we may even fear losing an acquired virtue. When meditating, some people are afraid of going into *samādhi* (a transcendental experience) for fear that they may not come back; or when having visions, they wonder if they will last. Thus, what we fear losing depends upon the grossness or subtlety of our mind.

There is also fear of the unknown; for that reason we want to find out what is in store for us in the future. This is why people are often afraid of spiritual life, because it is a mystery. We have relative knowledge of the subjects studied in medical or engineering colleges, but the search for God or Self-realization is unknown. If a person begins to attend spiritual discourses, his family and friends are afraid that he will lose interest in all material things, become a monk, and perhaps leave home. They may recognize that it is a good pursuit, but again they fear losing something. The fear of losing is because of attachment. The feeling that without a particular thing we are not complete, or that without it life is useless, is attachment. Even though we may have fewer possessions, we may still be afraid because of our attachment to them. Conversely, we may have immense wealth and be totally free from fear of losing it, like King Janaka. So, fear does not depend on how many things we own but on how attached we are to them. When there is no attachment, there is no fear. Deep within ourselves we already know that we will eventually lose everything. That is the nature of the world. Everything is bound by time. Thus, the great rishi Bhartrihari put it beautifully, "Dispassion (detachment) is fearlessness."

Following is an incident that actually happened to a secretary in India who worked for a large corporation. One day he said to me, "Sometimes management asks me to do things that I do not like. What should I do?" I said, "I will tell you, but please act at your own risk. Keep a resignation letter handy, and the next time they ask you to do something that you do not like, tell them that you will not do it and why. At most they can fire you, or perhaps they will ask if you are aware of the consequences. At that time give them the letter." Even though he was afraid he might lose his job, when the issue came up again, he actually gave his manager the resignation letter. Management's response was immediate; they invited him to discuss it, because they did not want to lose a trained and honest worker.

Another big source of fear is constant worry over what others will think of us. In this world of material pursuits, if there is a person who wants to dedicate his life to a social or spiritual cause, we often fear what people will say. When I came to America, people asked, "How can you wear those orange robes in America?" My reply was simple, "In America some people wear weird clothes and hair-dos, and if they disapprove of the way I dress, it is their problem. If people look at me, I also look at them, and that is all there is to it." The worry over thoughts such as, "What will people say? What will people think? What will happen?" are the cause for bondage to the world. A passage in *Nārada Bhakti Sūtra* says very beautifully that the one who uproots this kind of bondage to the world is the one who crosses over *māyā*. Once we are convinced that we are acting rightly, we should have no fear.

Let us now examine how we develop fear in reference to our actions. Scriptures contain many injunctions of do's and don'ts. If we do what we are supposed to do, and avoid what we are not supposed to do, then there is no fear. But when we perform a prohibited action, then fear follows naturally. The child who has not done his homework is afraid of the consequences. Therefore, not doing what we are supposed to do causes fear.

Fearlessness

Fearlessness (*abhayam*) is what we should strive for. Fearlessness is evident when: a) we are not attached to possessions, b) we are not attached to worldly name and fame, and c) we perform our duties and refrain from prohibited action.

There are two aspects to all virtues. If fearlessness is a virtue to strive for, the other aspect demands that we should let others be just as fearless and not instill fear in them. Some people are fearless themselves but their actions instill fear in others. In the consecration ceremony of *saṁnyāsa dīkṣā*, where one becomes a swami, he or she vows to proclaim to the world, "I am not afraid (of you) and you need not be afraid of me." It is a vow of renunciation and means, "If you want a certain object or being, please have it, I have no interest in it at all." That is called *abhayam* (fearlessness). No one is afraid of that person because he or she is not in competition with anyone. Whether one is attempting to become a spiritual giant or to follow in the footsteps of great scientists and explorers, without fearlessness we cannot progress.

How do we become fearless? We become fearless when our mind is without negativity and has pure motives. But as long as we have likes and dislikes, with their subsequent desires and attachments (*rajas* and *tamas*), negative thoughts will always tempt us. Purity of mind is a natural state of the mind. It is an expression of *sattva guṇa* (the *sāttvika* temperament). Our minds automatically glide into this natural state when we eradicate our mental impurities and gain true *sāttvika* knowledge. In a pure mind one can invoke and experience the divine presence of the Lord. Such a person develops sanctity or holiness, which is called *sattva saṁśuddhiḥ*.

Abidance in the Yoga of Knowledge

How can we attain those divine qualities? We can attain them through firm abidance in the path of Self-inquiry. Understanding the Truth will lead one to fearlessness and purity of mind. Incorrect understanding projects a false sense of security onto the objects of the world. Then we search for happiness and security in these objects where none can be found; and, as a result, we develop likes and dislikes. As soon as we recognize the problem, we begin to look for a solution. That solution is not found in chronological time and effort, but in right understanding.

Similarly, problems at the mental level cannot be solved by actions at the physical level. We cannot "do" something to get rid of anger or jealousy. If a room is dusty and dirty, we apply physical effort to clean it; but if a room is dark, then all the sweeping and dusting in the world will not rid us of the darkness. Yet as soon as we bring in light, the darkness is gone immediately. Darkness is not eliminated gradually; it disappears immediately. In the same way, once a person realizes that his thoughts are wrong, the transformation is immediate and complete. That is why in the fourth chapter of *Bhagavad Gītā*, Lord Krishna says that those purified by the penance of Knowledge come to Him.

We may wonder, "How long will it take to get rid of negativity?" No timeline can be given. Sometimes a whole lifetime is not enough to eliminate one's wrong tendencies. Yet history tells us of many people being transformed suddenly and totally, of ordinary people suddenly becoming saints. It is not a question of chronological time. Rather, these cases illustrate that men and women were transformed by their great determination. The quality of their determination brought about an immediate and extraordinary change in them.

A brilliant example is Swami Chinmayananda. He originally journeyed to the Himalayas as a secular journalist to expose the "bluff" of the swamis. However, he was so impressed by the wisdom, selflessness, and service of both Swami Sivananda and Swami Tapovanam that he stayed there to study with incredible determination. He himself was later transformed into one of the greatest spiritual Masters of our age.

For most of us the process is gradual. When we see that our mind is gradually shedding its impurities, we are encouraged and feel confident. It is not that all problems go away or negative thoughts do not arise. The difference is that we now understand from where they arise and we are aware of the whole play. They just do not affect us like before. Thus we become free from fear and worries.

III

The Psychology of Fear
by Swami Ishwarananda

Fear is psychological. Its expressions are seen both in physical and emotional layers of our personality. While psychologists and psychiatrists consider fear as a "disease," spiritual traditions consider fear as the main factor that drives one toward Wisdom. What is the psychology of fear?

Fear in context. Are you afraid of a tiger? Your answer will be NO, if the tiger in question is behind a cage in a zoo. But if it is in an open field, then your answer will be YES. So, what causes fear, the tiger? The answer depends on the context in which both you and the tiger are placed. One is afraid of a dreadful dream till one wakes up from it. The dream in context is fearful for the one who is unaware that he is dreaming!

Fearlessness is in changing the context. A suicide bomber is not afraid of death; he voluntarily invites death mainly because his context is different. He is convinced by his faith that death is a sacrifice and not suffering. His believing heart empowers him to face his physical death without any hesitation. Thus, with a change of context, a person can live without fear about death and all calamities, such as old age, disease, and suffering related to the physical body.

Fear of uncertainty. When one is not sure of the consequence of one's attachment, status, power, possession, relationship, and so on, he lives in fear. Fear is therefore not an outcome of any one of these, but surely the uncertainty of their sustenance. In a famous verse from *Vairāgya-shatakam,* Sage

Bhartrihari sings:

> Pleasure is accompanied with fear of disease; noble birth with a fear of possibility of a fall; wealth with fear of tax; dignity with misfortune; army with power of a strong enemy; beauty with old age; knowledge with controversy; merits with wicked people; body with death — all objects in this world are beset with fear. Dispassion alone is fearless!

Dispassion is the antidote for fear of uncertainty. Realizing the uncertainty of matter is dispassion. The practice of dispassion is to remind oneself again and again, and more than a practice, it is a realistic vision. Lord Krishna instructs his friend-student Arjuna, who questioned the fickle nature of the mind, "get hold of the mind through practice and dispassion."

Fear — a protector. Our body is subject to death, and fear protects us from engaging in situations that can harm the body. This defensive mechanism is in-built in all animals, which lack the intelligence to protect themselves from danger. Conversely, humans use their intelligence to save themselves from physical harm. Nations secure their boundaries with strong armies and ammunitions due to fear of insecurity to their land, wealth, and people.

Once there was fire in a house where a child was alone while the mother was in the backyard. She panicked and called the fire brigade. In spite of many warnings from the firefighters, the mother of the child jumped into the engulfing fire and brought her child to safety. Her courage was not due to her physical strength — it came from the protective instinct that prompted her to act without fear!

Fear of change. Change causes fear when one is habituated to a certain style of living. Many fear retirement from a busy professional life. In spite of the ongoing physical and emotional stress of a busy life, the fear that one will become unproductive drives one from pillar to post till death. Planning retirement, meditation, diet, and physical workouts are often neglected by such "busy" bodies mainly due to fear of change, which is baseless! Accepting and also inviting change with a smile is the antidote to this groundless fear. Change cannot be avoided, and rejecting the change only sustains one's insecurity and associated weaknesses.

Fear provides thrill and excitement. Most sports and adventures excite the players, performers, and audience, because the fear of failure or challenge creates a positive energy to achieve the goal and to overcome the challenge. One of the famous Everest climbers remarked: "I did not conquer a mountain; I conquered my mind by climbing this." It is the "fear factor" that keeps everyone excited, on edge, and living in the present while engaging in dangerous adventures and sports!

Fear supports faith. Most religious faiths are built on fear of God. It is believed by the ancients that the law of nature is abiding due to fear of God. A famous verse in the *Taittirīya Upaniṣad* (2:8.1) reads: "Out of His fear the wind blows. Out of fear the Sun rises. Out of His fear runs fire, as also Indra, and Death, the fifth." Most people go to places of worship or perform their daily rituals of prayer due to fear of a curse from the gods. Celebrations and religious observations have elements of fear attached to the faith. Superstitions are followed without question by many for generations, due to the inherent fear connected with the unknown.

Fear initiates search for immortality. Fear of death is the greatest fear in all. Search for immortality is to find an avenue to overcome this fear while living, also to discover that which is beyond death. The science of medicine has been attempting to conquer death by successfully increasing the longevity with the help of drugs, while spirituality's main forte is to demystify death.

In his book *Jonathan Livingston Seagull,* the famous author Richard Bach wrote: "Jonathan Seagull discovered that boredom and fear and anger are the reasons that a gull's life is so short, and with these gone from his thought, he lived a long, fine life indeed."

In *Bhaja Govindam*, a famous composition of Adi Shankaracharya, the opening verse indicates, "All human endeavors related to worldly prosperity do not save one from fear of death except devotion to God." Devotion that transforms one's identification from the limited to the limitless, from the finite to infinite, and from the mortal to the immortal is an antidote to the fear of death.

Fear caused by perception of differences. The main causes for both world wars were due to the fear of oppression of religious beliefs that lacked universal vision. Differences create fear. Many philosophers hold this view: *Opposite of Love is not hatred, it is fear!* Love unites — fear divides. Love sees Oneness while fear sustains difference. Vedanta, the science of life, emphasizes universal vision as fearlessness. "For, whenever a seeker (of Liberation) creates the slightest difference in It (*Brahman*), he is smitten with fear. Nevertheless, that very *Brahman* is a terror to the (unripe) learned man who lacks the vision of unity" (*Taittirīya Upaniṣad* 2:7.1)

So, is fear unnecessary?

On one occasion, the Buddha said to his disciples, "Behold monks, all beings have some kind of fear such as fear of death, sickness, old age, life after death, and so on."

When the Buddha finished his speech, one monk asked him, "Lord Buddha, is there anything more than those to be afraid of?"

The Buddha answered, "Yes, there is, monks, *avijja* (*avidyā*) ignorance darkens this very world. In the darkness of ignorance, there is no light of the sun and the moon."

Then he was asked for more explanation and he explained as follows:

1. Not knowing this body as the base of all attachment, which causes suffering; seeing suffering as happiness is the most fearful.
2. Not knowing the suffering sprung from the attachment to this body is the cause of suffering; seeing this body as a base of happiness, and so attaching to it.
3. Not knowing there is liberation from suffering; understanding that there is no way to be free from suffering and believing that one must suffer again and again, never escaping from suffering.

4. Not knowing the truth of things, or the cessation of suffering; being deluded into thinking that this way via (drink, drugs, materialism, etc.) is the cause of real happiness.

Be afraid of ignorance, without which there is no dawn of wisdom!

One of the scriptures of Judaism states:

He in whom the fear of sin comes before wisdom, his wisdom will endure; but he in whom wisdom comes before the fear of sin, his wisdom will not endure. (Mishnah, Abot 3.11).

IV

The Feeling of Fear
by Miriam Greenspan

Fear is as human as laughter and tears. Though few of us would care to admit it, we are all afraid. It gets down to this: the human condition is scary. Pain, loss, and death are guaranteed the moment we are born. So too is some degree of helplessness in the face of apparently random events over which we have no control. We fear uncertainty, helplessness, and isolation. We want to live without pain or death. And these impossible wishes make us all the more afraid. These basic existential fears inhabit us, whether we are aware of them or not. Almost any phobia or fear you can name, at its core, gets down to these six: fear of pain, loss, death, vulnerability, isolation, and chaos.

To a large degree, we live with these six basic fears without paying too much attention to them. Few of us walk around saying, "I'm scared of pain, loss, death, vulnerability, isolation, and chaos. What about you?" (not much of an opener for a cocktail party conversation). But there are times when fear comes knocking on your door and walks right in, uninvited: You are diagnosed with breast cancer. You lose your job in a down-sized economy. Your fourteen-year-old daughter has anorexia. A loved one is dying. When we are in the grip of unavoidable fear is when we have most to learn from it.

Fear arises in any situation where there is a threat of loss or harm to body, mind, and spirit. It is a basic emotion, built into the biological organism. Part of our deepest instinct for survival, fear is our emotional alarm system. Like the other dark emotions, it has an inherent intelligence. Without it, we would be unable to protect ourselves. Fear for those we love is often more intense than fear for ourselves — as any parent knows. Fear is part of the human glue that binds us to one another, in both helpful and harmful ways.

What fear tells us is that something requires immediate and close attention. Its purpose is to move us to action to protect life. An alarm signal goes off that says: Stop where you are — there's danger ahead. Get ready to fight or flee. The "fight or flight" response has, of course, changed over the centuries. We no longer throw our spears at wild buffalo or shimmy up a tree when our prey becomes predator. Still, there are other, less immediate, more complex, and yet frightfully dangerous elements to be attentive to in the interests of protecting life on earth. At perhaps no time in the history of the earth is fear a more appropriate emotion.

Fear as a Way of Knowing

Take a left here, says a still, small voice. Our rational mind may say, *No! I need to take a right.* Listening to the "irrational" voice, we narrowly avert a terrible car accident. Most of us have had some experience like this, a bolt of fear or queasy internal alarm that irrationally alerts us to a catastrophe waiting to happen or something urgent that requires our attention.

In a culture that dishonors the wisdom of emotion in general, and fear in particular, we're not likely to experience fear as a legitimate or rational emotion. We're even less likely to trust fear as an "irrational" way of knowing.

Yet consider the story of Adam Trombly. On a fine sunny day in the spring of 1974, Mr. Trombly, director of an environmental organization called Project Earth, was walking through a cow pasture in Rocky Flats, Colorado. Suddenly, he had a queasy feeling in his stomach. A feeling of fear and dread suffused his body, though it was a perfectly benign Sunday afternoon with cows grazing on the green grass. "There's something very, wrong here," Trombly thought, "and I'm going to try to find out what it is."

He had some soil samples taken from the ground and had them tested. It turned out that the soil was saturated with an invisible toxic substance. The level of plutonium oxide in the earth at this particular site was many thousands of times the acceptable level. There had been a major fire at Rocky Flats Nuclear Installation, and plutonium oxide had been released into the atmosphere. Though this was the worst nuclear accident in the history of the United States up to that point, it was unreported in the press. Trombly's fear "discovered" the problem — and the cover-up.

For most scientists, the idea that Adam Trombly took his fear as seriously as he would any bit of evidence, and acted accordingly, would appear to be ridiculous. Yet through trusting his emotional response, he was able to receive information from the earth itself. This is a way of feeling and knowing that our culture does not recognize, much less endorse and support. On the contrary, by any contemporary psychiatric assessment, Trombly's way of listening to fear would be called an "idea of reference." Ideas of reference — the sense that inanimate objects are talking to us, bringing messages to direct our actions — are considered to be symptoms of a psychotic thought disorder. From this standpoint, listening to fear of this kind as a potential source of information is delusional.

Conventional social science does not recognize intuition: the nonrational information that comes to us from the emotional part of the brain. Listening to fear and learning to discern the important information that it may be conveying is an important part of developing the "sixth sense."

Many years ago, for a number of months, I experienced a pronounced sense of dread and fear whenever I walked up the backstairs of my home. The feelings would intensify as I approached the second-floor landing. Having no idea why fear seemed to descend on me as I ascended the stairs, I began to worry that I was developing a new, heretofore unheard of phobia: fear of hallways. But it was only this specific hallway that triggered my fear — not your classic phobia. One day I spontaneously decided to "follow" my fear up the stairs like a

Geiger counter — to go where it led me. It led me to a pipe in the hallway, buried underneath a pile of old newspapers. As I removed the pile, I noticed that the pipe's white wrapping was flaking off onto the floor. This was years before "asbestos" became a household word; the home inspector had never warned me that this pipe, as well as many of the pipes in the basement of my home, were wrapped in asbestos insulation. Though I had no conscious knowledge of this toxic substance, my fear alarm went off with a loud blast as soon as I saw the white flakes in a little pile near the pipe. Believe it or not, the word "asbestos" actually came to me. I immediately called a company to come and check on it. Indeed, after a simple test, I was informed that asbestos was flaking off the pipe — and is most dangerous in its airborne form. I had it professionally removed. Inexplicably, my fear led me to discover this toxic substance in my home.

Don't be afraid to explore your fear — you never know where it could take you!

The Value of Irrational Fears

Right about now, you may be thinking: "But what about my fear of flying? of speaking in public? of intimacy? These feelings don't give me information. They're not prophetic. They're defeating, frustrating, and inhibiting."

It's true that many of our fears are groundless or neurotic. It wouldn't be particularly helpful to treat all our fears as though they were giving us accurate information. But this doesn't mean that our irrational fears are totally without value. The value of irrational fear is that it humbles us. It tells us we are human and less than perfect. It lets us know that we are in need of healing.

For example, your fear of abandonment may be irrational in the context of a solid marriage to a loving, devoted spouse. But it's still a signal. It tells you that you need to attend to some pain from the past. It alerts you to the fact that your heart needs to be healed if you are to grow in your capacity to give and receive love.

Your fear of abandonment may also carry some information about your partner's limitations. Perhaps your spouse cuts off emotionally when he's overwhelmed by feelings of his own. Your experience of his emotional cutoff as abandonment can teach him how his emotional withdrawal affects you, and lead him to inquire into his own fear of emotions. There is valuable information here for him too: Befriending his emotions would enlarge his capacity to connect to you.

Fear may be uncomfortable but it need not be a problem. The artist Georgia O'Keeffe said, "I've been afraid every day of my life, and I've never let it stop me from doing anything."

Remember: It's not fear but avoiding fear that leads to phobias. Because we are scared to feel fear, we avoid whatever triggers it. It's the avoidance that locks the phobia in place. Phobias are one result of fear when its energy is toxified by avoidance. For example, when you don't move off the sofa because you're afraid of going out and getting hit by a car, it's not fear that stops you; it's avoidance that stops you. Georgia O'Keeffe was not afraid of her fear, so it didn't hinder her in art or in life. She felt fear, but she wasn't phobic. If you are afraid of abandonment, this is not a problem unless you avoid relationships. You may be fearful of speaking in public, so you don't do it. You're afraid of flying, so you take the bus. It's not the fear that stops you. Its fear of *feeling* the fear that stops you. If you can feel it, you can heal it.

Psychologists call the capacity to feel an emotion "affect tolerance." When you are intolerant of fear, you avoid it. When you are tolerant of it, you can feel it and not let the feeling stop you. You can speak in public even if you're afraid you'll become tongue-tied. You can get on the plane and breathe through your fear. Fear is not the problem. Avoidance is the problem! If you can let yourself tolerate feeling fear, the feeling gradually decreases. Current programs of treatment for phobias are all based on increasing affect tolerance for fear through gradually increasing exposure to the phobic trigger. Steven Phillipson, clinical director of the Center for Cognitive-Behavioral Psychotherapy in New York City, puts it this way: When your fear tells you to avoid something "what you really need to do is face down the fear."[1]

The raw emotion of fear itself is actually not paralyzing but energizing. Fear moves us to act — and if we avoid instead, the fear only grows. The trick is knowing how to tolerate the potentially destabilizing energy of this powerful emotion, to face into it, and to find the right action.

Footnote:

[1]   Quoted in Jeffrey Kluger, "What Scares You?" *Time*, April 2, 2001, p. 62.

V

The Experience of Fear
by Rush W. Dozier, Jr.

At sixteen I was like every other teenager in America who had just gotten his driver's license. I wanted to joyride with my friends. The feeling of freedom and independence was delicious. The feeling of responsibility was less intense. Frankly, I'm amazed any of us survived to adulthood.

One Saturday night, five of us piled into my best friend's car. I was riding shotgun — sitting on the passenger side of the front seat. The summer night was soft and beautiful as we cruised along a country road through the corn and soybean fields of western Kentucky. Unexpectedly the car of another friend, also packed with teenagers, passed us going the other way. The second car slammed on its brakes and did a quick U-turn. The chase was on.

Our car accelerated down the narrow road, headed toward what seemed to be a gentle curve. At that speed it wasn't. Halfway through the curve we began drifting, out of control, off the road toward a high dirt embankment bordering a cornfield. The experience was terrifying. Time slowed down. As I stared out my window, the embankment seemed to move toward me in slow motion. I was frozen in my seat drenched in a sudden clammy sweat with an awful sinking feeling in the pit of my stomach. My pulse pounded in my ears. I was vividly aware of every blade of grass on that embankment.

With a loud bang, we hit. The car bounced in the air to the other side of the road and came to a stop. Everyone piled out.

Miraculously no one was even scratched. I can't say the same for the car. Over the next half hour we milled around in a daze, counting our blessings and waiting for my friend's father to drive out and take us home.

What I experienced was a classic fear reaction. Simply put; fear is the body's way of anticipating and avoiding pain and the danger's pain signals: injury and death. At that moment I thought I was going to die. A series of automatic physical changes designed to maximize my chances of survival took place in my body.

Much of my blood was immediately diverted to the large muscles, particularly my legs, so that I would have the maximum energy necessary for a quick escape. The draining of blood away from the skin produces the characteristic paleness of fear. Perspiration oozing out of my pale, cool skin produced the sensation of a cold sweat. The pounding I heard was my overwrought heart at work and my skyrocketing blood pressure.

Quick-energy hormones like adrenaline were pouring into my bloodstream and muscles. Sometimes this reaction goes awry and so much blood is diverted to the large muscles and away from the brain that a person faints. The odd feeling in my stomach was my digestive system contracting and turning off as all nonessential systems shut down in preparation for the escape.

The momentary feeling of being frozen in place is also a characteristic reaction to fear. Scientists believe this serves a variety of purposes. Most importantly, it forces you to concentrate on every possible avenue of escape. This concentration is accompanied by a dramatic sharpening of perception. stimulated by an instant flood of chemicals into the brain. The eyes widen and the pupils of the eyes expand to take in the maximum amount of information. In my case every detail of my surroundings came so sharply into focus that it seemed unreal. My very perception of time slowed. This kind of dramatic fear experience produces long-lasting and detailed memories. We remember best what threatens us most. Our survival depends on it. Several decades later I can still recall the event with startling clarity.

RUSH W. DOZIER JR.

The Most Primal Emotion

Fear is our most primal emotion. Evolution has wired our nervous system in such a way that intense fear takes precedence over everything else in our minds and bodies. When faced with a life-threatening danger, we instantly lose our desire for sex, food, or anything else other than to deal with the peril. Our reproductive system, digestive system, and all other secondary systems shut down almost instantly as the brain mobilizes the body for fight or flight. Fear is fundamental because life is fundamental. If we die, then everything else becomes irrelevant. Fear evolved in the earliest ancestors of all the animals living today. Virtually every type of animal, from fruit fly to monkey, experiences fear.

Charles Darwin was the first scientist to study the evolution of emotions systematically. In his 1872 classic *The Expressions of Emotions in Man and Animals* he concluded that "fear was expressed from an extremely remote period in almost the same manner as it now is by man...." The earliest ancestors of human beings dealt with danger and their enemies by "headlong flight, or by violently struggling with them; and such great exertions will have caused the heart to beat rapidly, the breathing to be hurried, the chest to heave, and the nostrils to be dilated." These responses to fear are part of our evolutionary heritage.

Fear is one of our most basic emotions. The word "emotion" comes from the Latin word *motere,* which means "to move." The word "motivation" has the same root. Patients with extensive brain damage that destroys their emotional centers often lose their motivation to carry on everyday activities and become apathetic, even catatonic. "Fear" is derived from the Old English word for danger. The emotion of fear has evolved to move us away from danger.

Because it is found in so many species, fear has become a premier window on the mysteries of the brain. It allows neuroscientists to study the fear circuits of animals with relatively simple brains and use this research to ferret out universal mechanisms, not just of fear but of all forms of memory, emotion, behavior, and learning. Other animals not only feel fear, they learn from it just as we do. In the laboratory, a rat can be taught to associate the sound of a bell with a mild electrical shock to its feet. Thereafter whenever the rat hears the bell it will freeze, fearing what is to follow, even if the shock never comes. The rat has learned to fear the bell. Researchers can study the rat's fear-conditioned brain to see what changes have accompanied this learning. Through understanding fear we understand ourselves.

VI

Breath and Fear
by Andy Caponigro

One who conquers others is strong; one who conquers himself is strongest. Lao Tzu

Mark Twain once quipped, "Everyone talks about the weather, but no one does anything about it." As a healer, I've noticed that everyone talks about fear but no one does much about it — mostly because they know little or nothing about how it's created or what it actually is. Most people think of fear as an inner enemy that must always be kept under control. For example, during the depths of the Great Depression, President Roosevelt made the famous statement "There is nothing to fear but fear itself." In the science fiction novel *Dune*, Paul (the hero) kept his mind steady in a crisis by reminding himself that "fear is the mind-killer." However, fear is neither an enemy nor a mind-killer; it is one of the most powerful and beneficial allies we can have in times of danger.

I once read a remarkable newspaper story about a mother who "miraculously" saved a trapped child from certain death by lifting a truck. At the time, I was a college student living in Boston, and the story came from the Midwest, but it stuck with me all these years. The newspaper account described how a three-year-old girl had become pinned under an overturned truck. Her mother, a slightly built woman, had single-handedly raised the truck enough for bystanders to pull the child to safety. When an astonished newspaper reporter asked the woman what made her even think of trying to lift the truck, she replied, "I never stopped to think for a moment. I was much too scared for my baby!" How did she do it? This heroic woman had inadvertently discovered some of the incredible powers that fear can bestow in moments of crisis. In order to consciously tap into these powers, however, we must first understand the true nature of fear.

Danger Consciousness

Fear is the emotion we experience whenever we think we're in danger. Pure fear — fear uncontaminated by anxiety — usually comes upon us suddenly, triggering a series of physiological changes that prepare our body for unusually intense forms of action. For example, a sudden rush of adrenaline causes our breath to speed up and our heart to beat faster. As the energies of fear course through our body, they quicken our reflexes and infuse our muscles with new feelings of strength. Although these sudden changes initially feel disconcerting because they are so intense, we must allow the energies of fear to flow through our system without resisting them, because they are the source of power that can enable a scared mother to lift a truck off her child.

The changes that take place in our mental processes are even more striking. Immediately after the energies of fear begin preparing our body for action, our mind becomes profoundly still and the world suddenly appears in slow motion. The rhythms of our breath and heart begin to slow down to match our calm and unhurried state of mind. Our body begins to feel steady, strong, and delicately poised for action, like a powerful lioness carefully stalking her prey.

It takes but a few seconds for our mind and body to enter this profoundly calm and one-pointed state, which I call "danger consciousness." Once we're in it, seemingly impossible tasks can be accomplished with ease. An American soldier who slipped into this state during a fierce battle in Vietnam found that he could easily sidestep the fire of a sniper; the bullets seemed to be coming toward him in slow motion.

This type of slow-motion perception has been reported by great warriors and martial artists of all cultures. For example, Chief Crazy Horse, the great American Indian warrior, was said to be virtually invincible during battle because he could consciously induce this state by meditating just before entering the fray.

Morihei Ueshiba, the great founder of the gentle martial art of Aikido, seems to have been permanently established in danger consciousness. For example, eyewitnesses have testified that Master Ueshiba could dodge bullets that were fired at him point-blank. Although he had once been rejected by the Japanese army for being too small, Ueshiba could perform prodigious feats of strength, such as moving enormous boulders with his bare hands or flattening a squad of attackers with a powerful shout.

Danger consciousness is a state of profound meditative absorption in whatever task is at hand. It enables us to experience the peace and stillness of deep meditation even though we're performing intense, dangerous physical actions in the outside world. Warriors who enter this state become virtually invincible because this slow-motion view of reality gives them an enormous advantage over any adversary who is still functioning in "normal" time. Great martial artists can enter this state at will and dispatch a surrounding band of attackers as if they had eyes in the back of their head. I've heard that some can even accomplish this feat while wearing a blindfold.

Breath, Fear, and Anxiety

Fear sends an urgent message to the mind and body: "Danger! Do something!" The way to tap into the extraordinary powers that fear can supply is to concentrate on the "Do something!" part of the message. Then, like Master Ueshiba or that heroic mother, we can move mountains. On the other hand, if we concentrate on the "Danger!" part of the message and become overly concerned with protecting ourselves, we tend to resist the energies of fear as they move through our mind and body in the mistaken belief that they're threatening our strength and stability. When we resist the empowering energies of fear, however, we transform them into the crippling energies of anxiety.

Despite what we've so often heard, fear does not "clutch at our heart." We do the clutching ourselves. When we get scared, we tend to hold our breath and we instinctively tighten our chest muscles to block the intense feelings that fear triggers in the region of our heart. This attempt to "get a grip on oneself" is actually a form of self-conflict that throws the rhythms and tensions of our breathing muscles out of synch with those of our heart. When we clutch in our chest to block feelings of fear, it not only creates anxiety, with all of its characteristic feelings of agitation, confusion, and paralysis, but it is also the cause of angina pectoris, which literally means "anxiety in the pectoral muscles."

Many people think that our heroes and heroines are fearless, but this is simply not true. They get scared, too, but they handle their fear better than the rest of us do. Contrary to public opinion, our heroes and heroines are not fearless; they are courageous. When courageous people become afraid, they don't close down on the flow of their breath to block their feelings of fear. They keep their breath open and flowing no matter how scared they are. We call such people "lionhearted" because they gracefully accept the intense feelings that fear triggers in the region of their chest and heart. This acceptance turns the energies of their fear into a powerful ally.

"Chickenhearted" people, on the other hand, are afraid to experience the symptoms of fear that show up in their mind and body. When they get scared, they resist these symptoms and try to control them by suppressing the flow of their breath. This frightened reaction to their own feelings of fear creates an energetic backlash that scatters their thoughts and actions like a flock of scared chickens. Fear never makes us feel weak or confused. The act of suppressing our breath to block and control our feelings of fear is what scatters our thoughts and weakens our actions. Thus, during the Great Depression, President Roosevelt might have more accurately said, "There is nothing to fear but *the fear of fear.*" And Paul, the hero of *Dune*, could have reminded himself that "anxiety (not fear) is the mind-killer."

It makes no difference whether our sense of fear has been triggered by an oncoming truck, a painful injury, a difficult emotion, or a traumatic memory. Whenever we use our breath to block our feelings of fear, we invariably create feelings of anxiety that remain trapped in our system and become part of our so-called subconscious mind. The sad truth is that what most of us usually call "fear" isn't true fear at all; it's anxiety. The even sadder truth is that most of us have scarcely experienced real fear since we were children. In those rare moments when we do feel real fear, it is quickly transformed into anxiety because our habit of clutching to suppress our fear has become so deep-rooted and automatic.

Breath, Strength, and Courage

Whenever we suppress our breathing to block feelings of fear, we create anxiety. To control this anxiety, we suppress our breathing even more — which causes us to feel more anxious than ever. When this vicious cycle spirals out of control, it leads to feelings of outright panic. Warriors from all cultures instinctively counteract this tendency to panic by shouting fierce war cries as they charge into battle. The war cries are partly intended to frighten their enemies, but more important, they counteract any tendency toward suppressing their breath in fear.

All great athletes and warriors are at least subconsciously aware of the breath's power to control pain and fear. As the going gets tougher, they intuitively tap into deeper reserves of strength and courage by changing the intensity, rhythm, and speed of their breathing. The exhilarating experience that runners call "second wind" is an example of how keeping the breath open, balanced, and flowing enables us to tap into these hidden reserves of energy. The Eastern martial artists brought this intuitive understanding to such high levels of conscious awareness that they were able to develop sophisticated systems of breath control for cultivating the virtues of strength, courage, and stamina that are essential to being a warrior.

Greatness of Spirit

Suppressing our breath to block feelings of fear not only creates anxiety, it also causes us to become discouraged — or "disspirited." Whenever we suppress our breathing to block feelings of fear, we weaken our connection with the spirit of life that strengthens and supports us. Greatness of spirit is the quality we most admire in our finest athletes and warriors. For example, great warriors are distinguished by the courage they display in the face of pain, fear, or even death. No matter how scared they get, they never lose touch with the spirit of life by suppressing their breath in fear.

By way of comparison, great saints and realized beings are distinguished not by their courageousness, but by their lack of fear, because they have completely transcended their fear of death. It takes courage to master our feelings of fear. It takes even greater amounts of courage to move beyond our sense of fear and lose our fear of death. Before we can become as fearless as our sages and saints, however, we must first have the courage of a warrior.

For example, Socrates was a famous warrior who became a great sage by graduating from the realms of sustained courageousness into the realms of fearlessness. As a young man, he was considered to be one of the most courageous and formidable soldiers ever to serve in the Athenian army. The turning point in his life occurred when he participated in an incredibly fierce battle that tested his strength and courage to their limits for three straight days and nights.

When the battle was over, Socrates climbed to the top of a nearby hill, leaned on his spear to support himself, then gazed across the battlefield in a trance-like state in which he stood motionless for twenty-four hours. By the time he turned to descend the hill, Socrates was no longer the courageous warrior who had fought in the recent battle. He had become transformed into the fearless sage who could remain calm and cheerful even while drinking a lethal cup of hemlock.

Mahatma Gandhi was a spiritual warrior who led his people to independence armed not with weapons of war, but with his sense of courage and his faith in God. Studying the career of this remarkable man is like retracing the footsteps of a saint in the making. Gandhi repeatedly jeopardized and eventually sacrificed his life to set his people free. By remaining courageous, no matter how much pain and fear he had to face to help his people, he became a saint-like being who transcended his fear of death.

Teresa of Avila was a "warrior-in-spirit" who became a saint by courageously surmounting incredible amounts of pain, fear, sickness, and self-doubt. Throughout her life, Teresa suffered from a relentless series of painful illnesses that tested her faith and courage beyond all limits of normal human endurance. Even her mystic experiences were often the cause of great personal torment. Teresa's inner experiences were so unique and beyond the ken of traditional Catholic doctrine, she sometimes feared they might be of the devil, or that she might be going mad. Even worse, if the Spanish Inquisitors had learned of her "unorthodox" experiences, they might have condemned her as a heretic. It was only Teresa's incredible sense of courage and faith in God that enabled this heroic soul to enter into rapturous states of Divine communion and transcend her fear of death.

Self-Mastery

In the Science fiction movie *The Empire Strikes Back*, Yoda tests Luke's courage and self-mastery by sending him into a dark, forbidding jungle swamp. When Luke inquires, "What is in there?" Yoda replies, "Only what you take with you." Within the swamp, Luke encounters his deepest fear in the form of a vision of Darth Vader — his greatest enemy. The lesson that Luke eventually learns is that self-mastery cannot be attained by confronting our fears and doing battle with them. This approach is destined to fail because we are the source of our feelings of fear. The harder we try to resist them, the weaker we'll get because we're fighting no one but our self.

This theme is also expressed in Paramahansa Yogananda's book *Autobiography of a Yogi*, in which he tells of meeting the "Tiger Swami" a Hindu monk who was famous throughout India for his ability to wrestle wild tigers and kill them with his bare hands. Repenting of his needless killing of tigers for the sake of riches and fame, the Tiger Swami eventually renounced his spectacular career to become a seeker of God. When the teenaged Yogananda praised the swami for being so brave as to wrestle wild tigers, the monk replied, "My son, fighting tigers is nothing compared to fighting the beasts of ignorance and fear that roam the jungles of the human mind."

These "beasts of ignorance" are nothing but the personal demons of fear that lie hidden away in the dark recesses of our minds. It is impossible to get rid of them by trying to fight them. Paradoxical as it may seem, the only way to cast these "demons" out of our mind is by learning to accept our feelings of fear whenever they show up. The "secret" to accepting our feelings of fear is to be courageous enough to feel them, and the key to accomplishing this lies in trusting the innate wisdom of the breath. If we keep our breath open and flowing — instead of closing it down in fear — the Divine Spirit that gives us life will always be there to support us.

In times of crisis, great saints and enlightened beings not only keep their breath open and flowing, but their breathing always stays calm and peaceful because they live in a permanent state of union with the spirit of God that dwells in their breath. This ability to keep their breath "as soft and gentle as a newborn babe's"[2] (in Lao Tzu's words) gives them the full protection and guidance of the Holy Spirit during times of crisis. This is why the Bible says:

> Though I walk through the valley of the shadow of death, I shall fear no evil, for Thou art with me.[3]

Each of us has the same inner tools for cultivating the virtues of strength, courage, and fearlessness as the great warriors and saints because our breath derives its powers from the same Divine source.

Footnotes:

[1]   Frank J. MacHovek, *The Book of Tao* (White Plains, N.Y.: Peter Pauper Press, 1962J), p. 5.
[2]   Ibid., p. 7.
[3]   Psalms 23:4 (AV).

VII

Remembered Wellness and Emotion

by Herbert Benson

Why is it important that we understand the role of fear and other emotions? Because remembered wellness is an emotionally charged memory, as are voodoo death and other examples of the nocebo effect. When we receive a diagnosis or a clean bill of health, our brains attach certain values to this news. And as it turns out, what we feel about the news may be far more important to the body's dispatch of signals about our health than an objective fact. When we hear about cancer survival rates, they may not register as strong an impression in our brains as the memory we have of a friend who lost all her hair and got very weak but eventually banished cancer from her body.

The vast conglomeration of nerve cells in the amygdala and other regions retains all sorts of memories and assigns emotions to those events based on the enormous history of life influences and experiences to which you have been exposed. If your contacts with the medical profession have been positive, you are apt to assign positive emotional reactions to receiving medical care, and the nerve cells involved in your neurosignature interact with other nerve cells in the brain to pass on and record their positive reading of the event. If on the other hand, in the case of voodoo, you are cursed by a witch doctor in whom you and the people in the village in which you have lived all your life have placed total faith, your fear may tragically trigger other neurosignatures to bring on sudden death.

Dr. Stephen M. Oppenheimer at the Johns Hopkins University Medical School has identified a small spot in the brain called the insular cortex that may be responsible for the sudden deaths often attributed to extreme fright, as happens in voodoo and crime victim deaths, and to those who are said to have died from "broken hearts." When activated by either extreme despair or panic, the insular cortex appears to cause heart damage, just as it does in people who suffer from a life-threatening heartbeat irregularity called ventricular fibrillation. With these two insights — the fact that top-down or thought-induced events are possible and that emotions work in the brain to assign priorities to events that are stored and recalled in neurosignatures — we may begin to understand the potential of remembered wellness and, conversely, of the nocebo effect.

Wiring and the Will to Live

Another important component in our understanding of remembered wellness, however, is the brain's ultimate priority, established in us even before we are born. This priority is to survive, the propensity for which we call "the will to live." We come into the world with some factory-installed elements, with some neurosignatures already instilled in our brains. This inborn wiring gives the body the guidelines it needs to thrive, to ensure blood and oxygen flow, immune system functioning, our perception of sights and sounds, and other basic survival mechanisms. This wiring is determined by our genes, by the contributions of the egg and sperm at the moment of our conception.

One of the specifics with which we are born is a fear of heights. In one example, infants have been placed on sheets of see-through plexiglass that are secured to the top of a dark table. Even though the plexiglass pane extends beyond the table on both sides and there are no perceivable tactile differences on the pane, the infants who are called to by their mothers will not crawl beyond the confines of the tabletop. They inherently understand the danger of the drop-off they perceive, even though the drop-off does not actually exist.

Among humans, the fear of snakes is almost as universal as the fear of heights. I am no stranger to this phenomenon. One autumn I planted tulip bulbs in the backyard only to be foiled by squirrels who kept digging them up. To frighten and deter the squirrels, I bought a six-foot inflatable plastic snake that, when positioned near the tulip bed, did the trick. But the next spring, after layers of snow had melted, leaving only layers of autumn leaves, I was raking the yard and unearthed my fake snake. Though it was a harmless impostor, it scared the living daylights out of me, and I shouted and leapt backward, only to be relieved that no one had seen me.

I owe this embarrassment to what some researchers call "hard wiring" — the traits with which we are born that seek to ensure survival. Scientists have argued for decades about whether the fear of snakes is hardwired or learned in life. Dr. Charles Pellegrino, an archaeologist and anthropologist, maintains that our fear of snakes is inborn, dating back to human mammal ancestors of 65 to 100 million years ago. These small mammals' major predators were huge snakes. According to Dr. Pellegrino, it is this innate fear that makes snake and dragon folklore common in so many different cultures.

Of course, psychiatrist Dr. Sigmund Freud suggested that snakes are phallic symbols and that our fears might be sexual in nature. But revisiting the debate in 1979, Dr. Edward J. Murray and Dr. Frank Foote of the University of Miami Department of Psychology issued a questionnaire to sixty college students to gauge their fear of snakes, their actual experiences with snakes, and the conditioning they received about snakes (that is, reading about or seeing films of snake attacks or witnessing fear of snakes in others). Drs. Murray and Foote learned that the greater the number of direct experiences the study participants had had with snakes, the less apt they were to fear the reptiles. And vice versa, the participants who had little or no direct experiences with snakes — the vast majority of the group — exhibited great fear of them.

Because the phobia was so prevalent and so rarely confirmed in reality, the investigators suggested that "a preparedness for developing a fear of snakes" exists among humans. We can speculate, as does Dr. Pellegrino, that because of the threat snakes posed for our distant ancestors, the brain is hardwired with the fear of snakes. As we have evolved, living in areas in which snakes represent less of a threat and reassured by the existence of venom kits, perhaps this neural instinct has diminished, leaving a less clear-cut impression. Nevertheless, this impression is easily manipulated and these fears are cultivated and promulgated in storytelling.

The Fight-or-Flight Response Revisited

The fight-or-flight response also appears to be hardwired. Nobel Prize-winner Dr. Walter R. Hess demonstrated that the fight-or-flight response was evoked by the stimulation of a portion of the brain, a discovery made in animals that is true in humans as well. We inherited from earlier generations the physiologic ability to fight effectively or run away from danger because our ancestors were unlikely to survive without it. Similar to the fear of snakes, even though our experiences of life may differ from those who came before us, we retain a genetic wisdom of the ages, designed to secure our future on earth.

We've long known that genes determine eye color and gender. And in what are sometimes unsettling revelations, science is rapidly identifying genes that make individuals and families vulnerable to certain cancers and diseases. But lately, genetic research has begun to assign predispositions in ways that seem to threaten our very notion of free will, suggesting that everything from sexual orientation to obesity, alcoholism to intelligence is biologically determined. We fear heights and snakes because our genes told us to do so. We have violent tendencies, some scientists have suggested, because of a deficiency of serotonin. Some of the differences between the sexes result from different ways in which men and women use their brains. And human emotions, personalities, even eccentricities and quirks appear to be nothing but the everyday excretions of an organism.

But lest you think that biology rules, that nature conquers nurture in that tired debate, here's a remarkable truth. The brain is malleable and changes constantly, millisecond after millisecond, according to our life experiences. Even though we are born with a set of instructions and neurosignatures, our brains perpetually recruit new nerve cells and nerve-cell activation patterns to handle its daily inputs — the cereal you eat at breakfast, a smile from your newborn, your rainy commute, and the deadlines and quotas expected of you at work. The minutiae of our lives are always absorbed and evaluated, our brains modifying themselves to handle whatever threats our lifestyles entail.

So not only is the brain the world's most efficient repository, a chronicler and librarian the efficiency and speed of which has yet to be even remotely mimicked by any computer; not only is the brain a trampoline from which springs all action and thought; not only are you endowed from the day you are born with survival instincts; but the brain is its own artist, its own chemist and engineer, constantly remaking and reconstituting itself. You are, at this very moment, a very different organism from the one you were seconds ago and the one you will be seconds from now. The decision-making structures of your brain direct all this traffic, not only relying on tried-and-true routes of nerve cell activation but designing new combinations of nerve cells and neurotransmitters to aid your survival and to help you learn new things.

Brain Plasticity

Scientists call this capacity for change "plasticity." A recent study demonstrated that rats raised in cages that featured toys and mazes grew more neural connections than did rats in empty cages. And thanks to brain plasticity, the same is true in humans. Drs. Avi Karni and Leslie Underleider of the National Institute of Mental Health conducted an experiment in which participants were asked to practice an exercise for ten minutes every day for several weeks: tapping their fingers sequentially — index finger to pinkie — on their thumb. The participants got quite good at it, doubling their speed and accuracy over the course of the four-week study. Periodically, the volunteers performed the finger-to-thumb exercise while having their brains scanned — this time by way of functional magnetic resonance imaging which enabled the investigators to identify the parts of the brain being used. Each time they received brain scans, the volunteers were also asked to perform the reverse sequence — pinkie to index finger — an activity they had not rehearsed.

On the scans conducted at the very start of the four-week study, Drs. Karni and Underleider found that the original and reversed sequence tasks produced the same-sized areas of activity in the area of the brain called the motor cortex. But after four weeks of rehearsing, the scan taken during the rehearsed sequence revealed an expanded hub of activity in the motor cortex greater than was present in the spontaneously performed task. The investigators concluded that repetition of the task, the frequent convening of particular like-minded nerve cells, recruited other nerve cells in the motor cortex, enlarging and changing the neural connections that were initially involved.

Much like the vocabulary we use to describe our computer hardware and software, our brains have hard wiring and soft wiring. We are hardwired to fear heights, probably snakes, and anything else that threatened the survival of our forefathers and mothers. We are hardwired to fight or flee and to rejuvenate ourselves with the relaxation response. But we also have adaptable wiring that enables us to learn new things and to practice new ways of thinking that can, over time, replace the patterns of thinking the brain was accustomed to inputting, evaluating, and acting upon.

All of us have distinct neurosignatures — for wellness, for illness, for strength and endurance, for headaches and nausea, for mobility and pleasure, for pain and disability, for the symptoms you associate with arthritis or angina, and for the specifics you associate with all the other activities and situations you have faced in life. Like a bad habit, or conversely like a good habit, recurring top-down thoughts, along with their corresponding emotional values, engage your brain's previously used nerve-cell-firing patterns to instruct the body. This is how our thoughts become self-fulfilling prophecies, and how our beliefs gear our bodies for the splendid opportunities of remembered wellness.

We cannot yet change our hardwired genetic predispositions and instincts by behavioral decisions alone, at least not in a time span that we, or our grandchildren, or even our grandchildren's grandchildren would be able to detect. And while genetic engineering may prove possible, the implications and ethics of altering our hard wires are another matter altogether. For now, let's accomplish everything we can by taking advantage of the marvelous malleability of our soft wirings.

When we change our minds, literally and figuratively, we can do a great deal to improve our health. Clearly our bodies and minds are composites of both genetic predispositions and adaptations inspired by our experiences. Nature and nurture are inseparable and interdependent, predestination and free will mingling naturally in our lives. Since both elements determine our neurosignatures — the very wirings of our brains that enable us to contemplate our bodies and our existence — the arguments over the dominance and superiority of either mind or body are ridiculous, their points moot.

PART TWO

Facing Fear: Step by Step

*If you do not come
face to face with your fears,
you will come to find yourself
always running away from them.*

Anonymous

Learn to redeem lower tendencies with emotions
and feelings of a higher order. We must cultivate the
habits of mental peace, cheerfulness, fearlessness,
and a general sense of contentment. When these
have taken root in us, we shall find desirable habits
displacing the old dissipating tendencies of anger,
worry, fear, and the sense of perpetual discontent.

Let us regularly open our head and heart to the enduring perfection and noble thoughts as preached
and lived by the wise noble seers of old. Such a con-
sistent exposure can strengthen and purify our character. By repression of false tendencies we can never
come out of their clutches; substitution of healthy
ideas alone is the way to grow in our character-girth
and personality-height dimension.

Swami Chinmayananda

VIII

Understanding
the Purpose of Fear
by Kathleen Fischer

When a huge tsunami devastated the coastline around the Indian Ocean the day after Christmas 2004, observers noticed a striking phenomenon. Almost no bodies of animals were found among those of the thousands of people killed by the giant walls of water. In Khao Lak, Thailand, elephants started trumpeting hours before the tsunami. They began wailing an hour beforehand, and just before it struck they fled to higher ground — some breaking their chains to do so. Similar animal behavior was reported in India, Sri Lanka, and Indonesia. Alert to the vibrating ground, to the sound and scent of the sea, and to the behavior of other animals, they sensed imminent danger and made their way to higher ground. Many humans, on the other hand, missed the signs or failed to grasp their implications. Some brought their children to the beach to watch the unusual behavior of the ocean.

The word *fear* initially evokes only painful associations, like those now linked to the tsunami. We seldom list fear among the things for which we are grateful. But as the tsunami disaster makes clear, fear arrives as blessing as well as burden. Animals (from fruit flies to monkeys) know fear. It tells them to flee or find shelter. So also with human beings. Designed as a natural warning system, fear helps us recognize and respond to anticipated peril. In fact, the word itself derives from an Old

English term for danger. It calls us to protect life, our own and that of others, and then to extend this protection outward to all creation.

The opening chapters of the biblical book of Genesis, in which we watch Adam and Eve being ejected from the Garden of Eden, contain an early account of human fear. Adam replies to God's voice, "I heard the sound of you in the garden, and I was afraid." By that point in the story, trusting relationships at every level have been fractured. In a world without sin and suffering, fear would presumably have no function. Life could thrive without the need to brace itself against possible threats. But the Book of Genesis depicts not only paradise unspoiled but also our current universe, Eden lost and not yet restored. Ours is a creation of lost innocence, riddled with danger, distrust, enmity, natural disasters, and therefore fear. Genesis is not the last time fear occurs in scripture; the Bible talks a lot about fear, telling us what to fear and what not to. Like the posters I recently saw on a Seattle bus, it reminds us both to "Look around. Be aware," and "Relax. Help is just a click away."

The immediacy and detail of worldwide communication today situates fear for our personal future within a broader horizon of global perils. We wonder about health, our own and our children's; we dread the consequences of environmental destruction, war and violence, epidemics, and biological and chemical terrorism. No conscious person could, or should, be entirely without fear in the face of such universal dangers. Like the flares at the site of a freeway accident, such warnings prompt us to prudence. In the past, fear has fueled many creative inventions that now enable us to avoid dangers. It will again prove to be a blessing if it leads us to change course and protect our planet's future.

Accepting Fear Rather Than Fighting It

A friend who has anxiously waited days for a doctor's decision about her breast biopsy finally learns there is nothing the matter with her. "I hope I never have to go through this again," she says as she comes out of the doctor's office. We know something of what she feels as she waits. Like her, we want to avoid feeling that way again if at all possible. It therefore puzzles us to learn that psychologists, Buddhist teachers, and other spiritual guides offer a similar recommendation regarding fear. The best way to deal with it, they say, is to allow it to simply be what it is. They use the terms *radical acceptance* or *befriending* for this nonjudgmental embrace of the body's reaction to danger. Psychologists term the ability to feel an emotion *affect tolerance*.

As with any of the emotions, denial complicates matters, dulling awareness in the same way a cataract clouds the pupil of the eye. Fear then often expresses itself as anger, a more socially acceptable emotion (especially for men). But if we convert the energy of fear to anger, we are likely to act out in destructive ways. As with experiences of referred pain, we do not realize the place that hurts is not the source of the trouble. The source lies somewhere else. Learning to face our fears with confidence that we can handle them creates a more direct and healthier path to what we want. With acceptance, there is room to recognize the information an emotion contains and then decide what we want to do about it. Listening to feelings in this way is the starting point for wise choices.

This implies that we need not be ashamed of being afraid. An Episcopal priest once told me about a retreat she made with other pastors. They were asked to step into a circle marked at various points with emotions such as anger, sadness, joy, and fear, and to stand wherever they most identified with a feeling. Almost none of them could acknowledge being afraid; it was too hard to ask for help and protection. Shame and embarrassment suggest that there is something wrong with us if we get scared. But Jesus himself knew fear, both in the Garden of Gethsemane, where he asked his disciples to stay with him, and earlier as he adhered to his own time frame for the final approach to Jerusalem, knowing his enemies awaited him there. The gospels even describe the bodily manifestations of his terror in the Garden, how he began to be "distressed and agitated" and told his disciples, "I am deeply grieved, even to death; remain here, and keep awake" (Mark 14:33-34). Seeing Jesus' fear is one of the ways we know he is human, and it confirms the fact that deep and powerful emotions do not signify weakness but rather reveal the full range of the human response to life's events.

Some past forms of spirituality fed this shame by valuing mind over body, and reason over emotion. They linked feelings such as anger and fear to weakness and also to fuzzy thinking. Today we realize that body and mind are closely intertwined, designed like an intricate piece of embroidery. Neuroscience is dissolving some of the mystery around our emotional life, and its breakthroughs enable us to understand fear perhaps better than any other emotion. Science tells us that feelings do not exist in opposition to reason; in fact, we cannot think well or make decisions without their help.

The Tibetan meditation teacher Pema Chödrön emphasizes that by acknowledging an emotion and allowing ourselves to feel the energy of the moment, we cultivate compassion for ourselves. This frees us to experience what scares us in a new way. I discovered the truth of her insight while healing from a fear of dogs that stemmed from a childhood incident. When I was ten, my sister and I were sent to a neighbor's house to pick up our weekly supply of eggs. What we did not know was that the neighbor was away and her dog was about to give birth to puppies. Instead of the welcome we usually received, we found an agitated and defensive dog that badly bit my little sister before I could stop it. I half-carried my sister home, and she had to be taken to the hospital.

Feeling responsible for what had happened and shaken by the upheaval it created, I developed a distrust of dogs I had never known before. A first step in facing this fear was letting go of the judgments I leveled against myself for feeling scared, as well as for the incident that led to it in the first place. Then I needed to gradually be around dogs. Sitting alone and avoiding them only increased my discomfort and solidified my bad memories. Over the years, learning more about their wonderful qualities from those who love dogs, being with them on walking paths and in the homes of friends, and finding that they come with varied personalities has helped me move through this fear. Without knowing my history, my clients themselves contributed to this healing as they brought their dogs in to meet me, shared their deep affection for them, or came to me in grief over the loss of a beloved pet.

Whether we call it radical acceptance or befriending, allowing ourselves to feel and face our fears takes courage. It does not happen easily. In fact, it requires grace. The Psalms repeatedly express trust that God will be with us in handling fear and moving beyond danger.

I lift up my eyes to the hills —
from where will my help come?
My help comes from the Lord,
who made heaven and earth.
                              Psalm 121:1-2

Many of the spiritual practices suggested in later chapters [The Author's *The Courage the Heart Desires*] lend support for this way of embracing fear and finding the courage we need.

When Fear Becomes a Problem

If fear is so valuable, why do we try to weed it out of our lives? Prolonged or misplaced fear shrinks the human capacity for joy, creativity, and freedom, making it impossible to fully realize the happiness God intends for us. Letting fear become a way of life also has negative physiological consequences. Fear sets in motion a sequence of bodily responses meant to help us escape danger. We cannot escape such responses altogether, and they sometimes serve a purpose. But if repeated or prolonged, they have serious consequences for health. As the brain centers that are crucial to fear keep registering potential danger, they set in motion a process that increases the body's stress hormones, which among other things makes the heart pump faster, quickens breathing, and reduces the ability to concentrate. This is helpful in an emergency, but if the body remains on this kind of alert, the stress takes a toll. It weakens the immune system and raises the risk of cardiovascular disease. The muscle tension created by anxiety produces headaches, insomnia, and back and neck pain. What was meant to be a life-saving resource now becomes itself a threat.

There are also more extreme forms of fear, conditions where fear has become pathological. Brain chemistry, genetic inheritance, childhood experiences, traumatic events, and current stress might all be causal factors. Think of these afflictions as the higher end of the fear spectrum, false alarms that cannot be turned off. They include severe trauma, panic attacks, and phobias. *Post-traumatic stress syndrome* is the term usually used for the psychological and physical difficulties that result from extreme trauma and stress, such as witnessing death or serious injury during war, or being sexually assaulted. The event is then relived in dreams, flashbacks, and other intrusive symptoms. A *panic attack is* a sudden bout of intense fear, marked physically by rapid heartbeat and shortness of breadth. A *phobia* refers to a specific fear, which may be of almost anything — heights, flying, strangers, public spaces, or closed spaces such as an elevator. Many people feel some mild fear of these things but continue to function normally. Severe phobias, however, can be incapacitating.

Dealing with serious forms of trauma, panic, phobia, or anxiety usually requires professional help, and sometimes medication. For many people, these kinds of fear involve great suffering and constitute a dark night of the soul. The good news is that there are many treatments available. Here too the spiritual dimension forms an important part of the healing process, as it strengthens and informs other approaches.

Most of us struggle with lesser forms of fear. Anxiety and worry gnaw at the edges of awareness, like a caterpillar munching away at leaves. In fact, ours has been called a culture of anxiety. Whereas fear is a limited emotion with a definite object, anxiety is an unfocused fear that reaches into all of life. Since human beings have the capacity not only to react to threats but to anticipate them as well, anxiety turns to what might happen in the future. Worry is the internal process of trying to figure out a way to escape from this potential threat. Worry often travels around with us, like a pebble in a shoe.

Anxiety is a painful and life-altering experience for those who endure it to any great degree. However, short of a serious anxiety disorder, we can often lessen it ourselves. Spiritual resources such as prayer and meditation offer powerful ways to better understand and reduce the impact of what frightens us. But fundamental to this weaving of spirituality into our experiences of fear is making sure that our spiritual beliefs themselves are not compounding the problem. This means, among other things, looking at how we understand fear of God.

Fear of the Lord

Many of us who grew up in an established religious tradition learned to fear God because of the ever-looming threat of hellfire and damnation. Such fear of God served as a disciplinary device in home, school, and church. It instilled in believers a dread of eternal punishment and made them uneasy about getting too close to God lest they be judged and found wanting. But using fear as a primary religious motive, along with failing to produce healthy spiritual lives, intensified the difficulty many people already had with handling their other anxieties. Gradually spirituality has shifted to a greater emphasis on the love of God.

Although underscoring divine love helps offset the negative impact of a preoccupation with sin and guilt, it can also lessen the sense of wonder and mystery vital to spirituality. In its root meaning, *fear* connotes alarm and dread, but also reverence and awe. It signifies amazement before this immense and complex cosmos and the divine Mystery that creates and sustains it. The Bible, in fact, often uses the phrase "fear of the Lord" to describe a deep reverence for God. This awe-filled attentiveness keeps us attuned not only to God's presence, but also to divine transcendence.

Scripture tells us that fear of the Lord comes as grace, a divine gift. When the prophet Isaiah promises that his defeated and demoralized people will have a new messianic leader, he declares that the spirit will rest on this person. It will be, *The spirit of counsel and might, the spirit of knowledge and the fear of the Lord.* (Isaiah 11:2-3)

Then, contradicting much of what we may have been taught about fear of God, Isaiah asserts that this spirit-conferred fear will be a delight. What can this possibly mean? It indicates that such fear does not preclude love and intimacy, as human fear might. Rather, it is love that leads a person to hold God in awe. Joy and delight follow.

Further, the recognition of divine Wisdom that flows from reverence allows us to release the heavy burden of believing we have sole responsibility for, and control over, everything that happens in the universe. Instead, trust in the divine Presence that upholds all creation puts our fears in perspective. This is why biblical figures are offered two seemingly contradictory statements: "The fear of the Lord is the beginning of wisdom" and "Fear not, for I will be with you." They are told what to fear and what not to fear. Trust in the mystery of God is fundamental to overcoming their fears.

Consider also the conversation Job has with God while trying to wrench some meaning from his immense suffering. After Job has fully laid out his bitterness and despair, God speaks to him in stanza after stanza of astonishingly beautiful poetry. God offers Job an extended hymn to the universe, a sweeping vision of Creation. Verse upon verse name the wonders of the universe: teeming seas and shifting rhythms of light and darkness, drops of dew and wildly flapping ostrich wings, soaring hawks and horses leaping like locusts. God asks Job,

> Where were you when I laid the foundation of the earth?
> Tell me, if you have understanding.
> …
> On what were its bases sunk,
> or who laid its cornerstone
> when the morning stars sang together
> and all the heavenly beings shouted for joy?
> …
> What is the way to the place, where the light is distributed,
> or where the east wind is scattered upon the earth!
> Job 38:4, 6-7, 24

Job's lesson in awe does not preclude a close personal relationship with God. Even as he acknowledges wonders he cannot fully grasp, Job experiences God's presence as the only real answer to his agonized questions about evil: "I had heard of you by the hearing of the ear, but now my eye sees you" (42:5). The Book of Job ends by affirming worship and intimacy as moments in the spiritual life, linked by an accurate understanding of fear of God.

Fear of the Lord, then, should produce not human cowering but true security, for it witnesses to a Wisdom beyond what we can immediately discern. As a central teaching of both the Bible and the Koran, this fear is not a debilitating anxiety; rather, it is a deep reverence for God that brings openness to divine guidance. When developed to its fullest extent, the fear of the Lord becomes the ideal attitude of a human being before the Creator, almost synonymous with faith itself. One translation of the Koran renders "fear of the Lord" as "God-consciousness." A person who "fears the Lord" in this fullest sense remains ever aware of the divine purpose in the universe. Fulfilling God's desire then increasingly directs one's life.

Fear's many cadences culminate in this reverence and wonder before the Mystery that sustains us. We have seen how varied fear's manifestations can be, from clear and appropriate fear that helps us avoid danger to nameless anxiety that plagues our days, and to troubling phobias that seriously constrict us. Understanding the purpose of fear and the shapes it takes helps us determine what to fear and what not to fear.

IX

Chant Away Your Fear

by Swami Swaroopananda

When we abide in Truth, we are abiding in our own nature, which is fearlessness. When we are ignorant of our true nature there is fear. Ignorance causes us to see duality hence there is fear of the other. The false ego lives in fear of the unknown, in fear of the possibility of sorrow, the invariability of change, and the surety of death. All anxiety, worry, insecurity, stress, and other forms of fear arise from these basic fears.

We experience sorrow and the fear of it, seemingly from three sources *ādhidaivika* — cosmic forces; *ādhibhautika* — neighbouring sources; and *ādhyātmika* — from within oneself. Though one may think one has no control over external forces, especially cosmic forces such as earthquakes and so on, our right attitudes to these sources will not only minimize the sorrow but also avert it totally.

The world is a projection of our mind. According to the *Bhagavad Gītā*; "As our faith, so is our mind." It is clear that those who strongly believe in goodness will experience good, and others, who have a negative bend of mind, will experience agitation in the very same situation. All our experiences are due to our belief patterns as well as our fears. Our belief patterns are created according to our reactions to life situations. Hence, if with proper knowledge we cultivate the right attitude towards situations, we will have nothing to fear.

When fear envelops us for any reason, remembering that someone more powerful is protecting us can console us. For example, a fearful child is immediately calmed by the mere presence of her parents. In the same way, when we have faith in a higher power or God, we are able to manage fear more diligently. All prayers, chants, and hymns help us to cultivate this faith and calm our minds to confront or manage the fear. Corporate journals report that people who have strong faith in some higher power deal with crisis much better.

Powerful Mantras and Chants

Certain prayers or chants are very powerful in helping eliminate fear. Mantras have many facets and help us in different ways at different levels.

First, there is the mystic power of their vibrations. We have experienced the effect of music in horror movies as well as the soothing effect of nature's songs. As thoughts of the mind are also vibrations, when we are able to make our mind vibrate with a different frequency the thought patterns and emotions of the mind change. In the same way, certain mantras when repeated change the vibration of our mind from fearful to confident.

Second, mantras create a certain positive mood, which replace our negative fears. The devotion that is manifested in the heart increases our faith and hence the qualities of hope, confidence, and fearlessness.

Third, in the mantra itself is encapsulated the knowledge and wisdom that removes our ignorance and hence the fear.

One such Vedic mantra is the *Mṛtuñjaya mantra* that helps us ward of the fear of death or even face death without fear.

Om Tryambakam yajāmahe sugandhim puṣṭi vardhanam
urvārukamiva bandhnāt mṛtyor-mokṣīya māmṛtāt.

We worship Shiva the Lord with three eyes,
who is fragrant and nourishes all beings.
May He liberate us from death, for the sake of immortality;
As the cucumber is automatically liberated,
from its bondage from the creeper (when fully ripened).

This mantra is chanted not only to ward off diseases, the possibility of untimely death, but also fear of death and the insecurities and anxieties of change. In its simple meaning it is a prayer to the Lord of death who has three eyes. The third eye — representing compassion and wisdom — points out that death is not merciless, but is compassionate; it liberates us. Death is pictured here as something that is effortless, like the severance of a ripe cucumber from the creeper, where the creeper itself detaches from the fruit and frees it. It also implies that fear and sorrow of death is due to our attachments. When we are free of attachment, death of the body is an effortless painless separation of the eternal soul from the perishing body, like ripe fruit freed from the creeper. When there is the ripeness or maturity of dispassion (*vairāgya*), death is nothing to fear. The death of the ego, in fact, is liberation and bliss.

Another beautiful and powerful chant or prayer is *Śrī Hanumāna Cālīsā* composed by Goswami Tulasidas. Hanuman, the devotee of Shri Ram, is the deity of strength, valor, wisdom, and devotion. All deities subjectively are our greater potentials or powers and faculty of the mind. When we invoke them we release the potential of our mind. The prayer is to remind us of our potential and what we need to cultivate in order to manifest it.

Where there is negativity and impure intentions in the mind, there is bound to be fear. Hence, the first verse of *Śrī Hanumāna Cālīsā* invokes the blessings of the guru to purify one's mind with the dust of the lotus feet of the spiritual teacher. Humility is the destroyer of ego, the cause of fear.

A situation becomes daunting when we do not have the strength to bear it nor the understanding to make the right decision, or the wisdom to act appropriately. Thus in the second verse the devotee prays to Hanumanji, who is the abode of strength, knowledge, and virtues, to give us strength, intelligence, and wisdom. Fortified with these qualities, we find that there is nothing to fear.

The different names, virtues, and feats performed by Hanumanji that follow in many verses give us the reverence, trust, and faith that a benevolent Lord is there to protect us at all times. They also point out all the essentials for living a fearless life. The mystic power of the chant promises to free one from all problems, difficulties, illnesses, pain, sorrow, and even negative psychic forces. Even death becomes liberating, and rebirth is to live a blissful life full of love and devotion.

Calamities from cosmic forces (*ādhidaivika tāpa*), that seem not to be under our control are also pacified with these chants. In India, in spite of the recent tsunami and various floods, a number of places of worship near the shore were not affected in spite of the devastating impact of the surrounding waters.

Sorrow from surroundings (*ādhibhautika tāpa*), are conquered through our love, dedication, compassion, and acceptance. Hanumanji's life shows how he surmounted all obstacles, confronted all challenges confidently while focusing on his goal, with faith in his heart, and attained success in all his endeavors.

Sorrows — such as illness, anxiety, guilt, and confusions — from our own equipments of the body, mind, and intellect (*ādhyātmika tāpa*), are conquered by surrendering with faith and devotion. Knowing that the Lord is all benevolent, all-knowing, and all-powerful. And that He is always forgiving, guiding, and protecting us.

In *Śrī Hanumāna Cālīsā* the devotee confidently declares to one's own mind: "With You as my loving protector, why should I fear anything" (*Tuma rakṣaka kāhū ko ḍarnā*).

Prayer done with faith calms the mind to deal with fear. Following the instructions in them gives us solution to remove fear. Abidance in the Truth through contemplation on the inner significance of the chant makes us fearless.

X

Let God Worry About It
by Susan Jeffers

> Good morning, this is God. I will be handling your problems
> today. I do not need your help. Have a good day. God[1]

I suspect that even if we received the above message directly
from the Source in all of His or Her glory, we would still feel
compelled to step in and take control, control freaks that we
are. Oh, wouldn't it be wonderful to have the trust that God in
His heaven is handling our problems today and every day of
our lives?

What about you? Do you believe in God? If you are like so
many students who have attended my various seminars about
overcoming fear, you would answer this question with an emphatic "Yes!" My next question would then be, "If you truly
believe in God, then why are you afraid?" And, again, if you are
like so many of my students, there would be a look of confusion
on your face.

Perhaps a more telling question would have been, "Do
you trust God?" I don't think there would have been as many
emphatic yesses in the room! The truth is that although the
American dollar bill says, "In God We Trust," there are few
Americans, or, for that matter, few people in the Western world,
who truly put their trust in God. *Belief* and *trust* are two very
different things.

Of course, you may be someone who simply has no belief
or trust in God whatsoever. There are many people who don't.
This is neither good nor bad. However, I can't help but feel

that it would take a lot of weight off your shoulders to believe in and trust something "bigger" than yourself. I don't know anyone who wouldn't like some "higher help" while walking through this fascinating and often difficult maze called life. And between you and me, if we look around, how can we deny the existence of *something* out there ... a Higher Power, a Universal force, Universal Light, or Universal Intelligence ... that creates the miracle of this world and the miracle of life itself? The thirteenth-century philosopher Rumi observed that ...

> When we talk about God, we're like a school of fish, discussing the possible existence of the sea.[2]

There is just too much that nourishes and supports us to deny the existence of *something* ... whatever that something is. Trust in a Higher Power is not a necessary ingredient for a beautiful life, but it is very valuable in helping us embrace all the uncertainty we face throughout our lives. ...

Even if you have absolutely no belief in God in the traditional sense, I would like to present various ways of trusting in some form of higher power in the hope that it may ease your worry about all the uncertainty in the world and give you comfort.

The "Tap Into the Light" Exercise

You may be wondering what my personal concept of a Higher Power is. A little background: I am Jewish by birth and pulled away from my religion in my teens because of the prejudice and righteousness I saw in those who had an "our way is the right way" kind of attitude. Of course, I noticed that this prejudice encompassed not only those who practiced my religion but all other religions as well. As I pulled away, I became free to embrace what is most loving in all religions and philosophies and let the rest go. While this may or may not be right for others, it has worked beautifully for me.

Even though I am not a religious person, I have a strong belief in a Higher Power. I experience it as a healing radiant

Light that surrounds the entire Universe. This Universal Light is always there for me (and everyone else) to tap into. I find that when I tap into this Light, I draw into myself the most positive energy one can imagine. In this powerful energy, I know there is nothing to fear. Obviously, it serves me well to remember to tap into the Universal Light on a constant basis!

How did I come to this way of experiencing a Higher Power? When I was young I pictured God as a man in white robes with a long white beard who was there to answer my prayers. I must say he was terribly inconsistent. Sometimes he answered my prayers and sometimes he didn't! Given his inconsistency, I was woefully confused about it all. And as I grew into adulthood, I was unsure whether I believed in God or not. But then one day something happened that convinced me that God was absolutely there for me, but not in the "form" I had previously imagined.

I had, sadly, just separated from my first husband and decided to take a vacation in Spain to clear my head. Having been very dependent on my husband, I was filled with great trepidation about traveling without him, but I felt the fear and did it anyway. (This was long before I wrote the book!) As I stood alone one morning in the garden of the Alhambra looking at the beauty around me, I was suddenly bathed in an overwhelming radiant Light that seemed to have come from nowhere. I felt myself blissfully dissolving into the oneness of the Universe and into a sublime sense of peace and safety. It was as if the Light had embraced me and told me without any words being spoken that I had nothing to fear.

This mystical experience lasted only a few moments, but I knew I had touched a new dimension of my being, a part of me that was able to connect with a Higher Power ... and my Spiritual Journey had begun. No longer did I envision God as a man in white robes with a long white beard who was there to answer my prayers. From that moment on, I saw God as a powerful, healing Light that is there *whenever I remember to tap into it.* This means that whenever I find myself bogged down in Lower Self thinking, I only have to close my eyes and imagine the

Light all around and within me. I am immediately transported to a Higher Self frame of mind, and all is well. Heaven!

Out of curiosity, I asked a dear friend over lunch how she "sees" God. She answered that she sees God in the form of a benevolent father who watches over us and fills the world with beauty. She says that her confusion lies in the horrors of the world. How could God allow such horror to exist?

Obviously, she is not alone in her confusion. Many have great difficulty in believing in God because of all the horrors in the world. I recently saw a satirical article which explained that God MUST have "bipolar disorder"! Bipolar disorder is a severe psychological problem characterized by cycles of depression that are awful for the sufferer and his loved ones and cycles of elation that are wonderful for the sufferer and his loved ones. What else could it be?

I told my friend about this article and we both had a good laugh. I then told her my concept ... that it's not a matter of God coming down and guiding us; rather, it's about our reaching up and pulling into our being the peace and power and love and learning that are always there for the taking.

Let me share with you one way I have devised for myself to tap into the Light. The only thing you need for this exercise is the great power of your imagination.

> First close your eyes.
>
> Then, in your mind's eye, imagine a magnificent all-encompassing Light, with the radiance of the sun, that envelops the entire Earth. Imagine it to be a Universal Light of healing, health, love, joy, and all good things.
>
> Then, take a deep breath and instead of exhaling through your mouth or nose, exhale by pushing your breath through a large imaginary hole at the top of your head. Visualize your breath shooting upward and connecting with the radiance of the Universal Light.
>
> Then visualize yourself inhaling this magnificent Light, again through the top of your head. Feel the Light filling your entire body and radiating outward

through your pores touching the world around you.

Keep repeating this process until you feel a sense of peace and strength and love.

My friend tried this exercise and loved it. I suggest that you try it as well. I suspect you, too, will love the feeling of the radiant Light of the Universe flowing throughout your being. It is a feeling that gives you the confidence that you can handle whatever life hands you. And it is very reassuring that this radiant Light is yours for the taking. Most of us walk around with a cloud over our head. It's time now to walk around with a radiant glow around and within us. It makes all the difference in the world.

The "Send the Light" Exercise

As we bring the Light of a Higher Power into and around ourselves, we can also send this healing Light to others. I do this all the time. I send Light to those who are ill or hurting in any way. I send Light to strangers who seem to be having problems in life. I send Light to those I love. I send Light to those who have made me angry (and soon I'm not angry anymore). When I send Light to others, I feel a sense of closeness and connection. Can you imagine a whole world of people sending love and Light to one another? Beautiful.

How do you send the Light to others? Simply alter the above exercise as follows:

Close your eyes.

Then, in your mind's eye, imagine a magnificent all-encompassing Light, with the radiance of the sun that envelops the entire Earth. Imagine it to be a Universal Light of healing, health, love, joy, and all good things.

Then, take a deep breath and instead of exhaling through your mouth or nose, exhale by pushing your breath through a large imaginary hole at the top of your head. Visualize your breath shooting upward and connecting with the radiance of the Universal Light.

Then visualize yourself inhaling this magnificent Light, again through the top of your head. Feel the Light filling your entire body and radiating outward through your breath and through your pores all the way to the person of your choice.

In your mind's eye, see the Light encompassing the both of you, creating a feeling of healing, love, and caring.

Bathe in this wondrous Light together and watch the love grow and any walls that are there come tumbling down.

Sometimes you may stand apart, sometimes you may hug, sometimes you may cry. In any case, a wonderful feeling of connection is established.

I have found this practice of sending radiant Light to others a very healing thing to do. I don't know if it's healing to them, but it certainly is to me! I believe you will find it healing as well. So whether you believe in this form of a Higher Power or not, I urge you to try sending Light to others.

Ultimately you can do this exercise with your eyes wide open. You will find yourself sending Light when entering a roomful of strangers, when enjoying a family dinner, when walking down the street, when in an interview ... everywhere! I find it incredibly useful to send this warming Light to my audience as I begin a workshop. I immediately feel connected. This blissful connection certainly feels better than when my knees used to knock and fear enveloped my entire being! So try sending this wonderful healing Light to those around you. It is an awesome form of connection.

The "Turn It Over" Exercise

This is an exercise that helps us to build trust in a Higher Power. As I said earlier, believing is not enough. Learning to trust is the essential ingredient. That's where we usually fall short.

If we try to control everything on our own (which, of course, we can't), we get very weary and very discouraged and very frightened. Once we can feel comfortable turning our worries over to a Higher Power in whatever form that feels right for us, we feel the weight of our world being lifted from our shoulders. In effect, we say to ourselves, "Take over, God. I trust it's all happening perfectly." This is our acknowledgment that we can't see the bigger picture, the Grand Design, and we really don't have any control over so many outcomes in our life. This kind of "surrender" is a tremendous relief.

The way I have used this exercise is as follows: When I find myself worrying about something in my life, such as money, a speaking engagement, one of my children, flying in a plane, or world events, I am quick to realize that I am forgetting to turn my problems over to a Higher Power. When I realize the problem ...

> I close my eyes.
> Then cut an imaginary cord that is attaching me to whatever I am worrying about.
> I then say to myself, "Okay, God, I am doing my best. I'll let you take over now."
> I take a deep breath and feel myself letting go (this step is very important).

As I turn my problem over in this way, I feel an immediate sense of relief.

Certainly the key here is to *remember* to turn it over, which is why I have always stressed repetition of the exercises I present to you. Our ultimate goal is to remember this exercise very early in the worrying game so that the minute a worry enters our mind, we can immediately cut the cord to the worry and "let God worry about it."

One of the pitfalls is that so many of us are able to turn it over, but then we take it back, and the worry begins anew. We, then, have to again remind ourselves, for as many times as it takes, that it's time to let God worry about it instead of allowing it to drive us crazy.

Another pitfall is that we selectively trust. "Oh, I'll trust God with this, but not that. I'll trust God with my finding a husband (or wife), but I won't trust God with my money ... no way!" This is one arena where we have to learn how *to go all the way in* order to find the peace we are looking for.

So we need to keep practicing and practicing and practicing until turning it over becomes an automatic action. Even then, we never stop the practicing. There's always the part of us, the Lower Self, that wants to take control.

The Lower Self doesn't trust anyone or anything, including itself, which is why it worries so much. It is in the Higher Self that our ability to trust lies. And when the Higher Self meets a Higher Power ... WOW! It is then that we are in touch with the incredible strength that we have to handle all that life hands us. There is no greater security than that.

It serves us all to make the decision every morning "to turn it over" before we even open our eyes ... before we start feeling torn apart by the difficulties that life is handing us. When we are able to turn it over, we make lots of room in our minds to think in a way that is courageous, loving, satisfying, and joyous. Not a bad way to go through the day!

The "Perfect Prayer" Exercise

Prayer is a valuable way of helping us to embrace uncertainty. So I strongly suggest that you give prayer a try. The healing effects of prayer, *even for those who do not believe in God,* have been documented in a number of scientific studies.[3] So even if you don't believe in God, pray to the Spirit or Higher Self within or simply to the Grand Mystery of it all, but don't negate the potential power of prayer in your life.

Perhaps you have been disappointed by prayer in the past. If so, it is almost a guarantee that your prayers were of the "petitionary" type ... that is they asked for something to be a certain way ... *your way, not God's way.* Sometimes petitionary prayers are answered; but often they are not. For example, when I was young, I prayed that my parents would live forever. Well, they didn't live forever. Obviously, this is a prayer that could never be answered. Yes, they are alive in Spirit and in my memories, but I wanted them to always be *physically* present so I could give them a big hug and a kiss. It doesn't work that way.

We have to learn to pray not with a sense of wishing, hoping, yearning, or entitlement, but with a sense of trust, gratitude, and purpose. If you don't know such a prayer, you're in luck! *In End the Struggle and Dance with Life,* I presented such a prayer which I will repeat for you now.[4] ("Thank you, Susan.") It is a prayer that will never let you down. Slowly, read it aloud right now, and feel the words enter your being ...

> Dear God. I trust that no matter what happens in my life, it is for my highest good. And no matter what happens in the lives of those I love, it is for their highest good. From all things you put before us, we shall become stronger and more loving people. I am grateful for all the beauty and opportunity you put into my life. And in all that I do, I shall seek to be a channel for your love.

How could you ever be disappointed with a prayer like that? No expectations, only a sense of trust and gratitude and purpose. If we began and ended every day with this prayer, and "lived it" throughout the day, the quality of our lives would improve dramatically.

I suggest you keep a copy of this prayer in your wallet, beside your bed, on your desk, and wherever you feel it will be noticed. Just keep repeating it over and over again until you memorize it. It is a prayer that will bring you peace.

The "Love Connection" Exercise

If you truly want to FEEL a sense of God, whether you believe in God or not, take notice of how you FEEL when you act in loving ways. It is a feeling like none other. Sublime. It is a feeling of connection and happiness in its purest form. Symbolically, it is truly embracing the Light of a Higher Power and letting it flow through you to embrace others.

Let me tell you about an interesting experience I had the other day that illustrates this beautifully. Impulsively, I did something very loving for a needy stranger. She looked at me in shock and surprise, and exclaimed, "Are you an angel? I just know that God sent you to me." I answered, "No, I'm not an angel, but maybe God did send me to you. After all, how come I showed up just when you needed me?" And I thought to myself, *Why did I show up at just the right time? Coincidence? Maybe. Maybe not! Who knows?* But I certainly feel that when we act in loving ways, the Light of a Higher Power is working through us. And it does feel sublime. So even if you don't believe in God in the traditional sense, perhaps you could embrace the concept of God as Love coming through us. To me, concepts of God and Love are interchangeable.

There is no question that all the bells and hoops and ceremonies and rituals, the robes and statues, and incense and gongs, found in our houses of worship create a very appealing atmosphere. And the tradition of going to our church or temple or mosque once a week or more can be a great reminder as to what it's all about (and we certainly need reminders!). It is important, however, in the middle of all the fanfare, that we don't lose sight of WHY we are sitting in a house of worship to begin with … and *that is to help keep us on the path* of *Love.*

Obviously, one does not need a house of worship to be able to stay on the path of Love. So whether you belong to an organized religion or not, you need to ask yourself the following question as you go through each day …

How can I be more loving here?

And, of course, follow up with appropriate action. As you fill your consciousness with loving thoughts and you act in loving ways, you are allowing the Love of God, the Force, the Light, or whatever it is for you to flow through you. As you experience this flow of Love, you will discover a sense of peace and fulfillment unlike anything you have experienced before.

Let me end this chapter by saying that all of the above are ideas and suggestions based on my own experiences. There is no right or wrong way to believe in God. We all have to experience a Higher Power (or not) in a way that is most comfortable and reassuring to us. If it is in the form of an old man with a white beard and flowing robes that's fine. If it is in the form of a woman sending loving energy throughout the world, that's fine. If it is in the form of Universal Energy, Universal Light, the Grand Design, the Force, or whatever, that's fine.

But whether you believe in a Higher Power or not, I suggest you just look with wonder at the Great Mystery of it all, and, with thanks, stand in awe.

Footnotes:

[1] Source unknown.

[2] I suggest you read the beautifully illustrated and moving book, *The Illuminated Rumi*. Translations and Commentary by Coleman Barks, Illuminations by Michael Green, Broadway Books, 1997.

[3] Larry Dossey, M.D., provides compelling evidence about the power of prayer in *Healing Words: The Power of Prayer and the Practice of Medicine*. HarperSanFrancisco, 1993.

[4] *End the Struggle and Dance with Life,* p. 181.

XI

Overcoming the Worry Habit
by Swami Chinmayananda

Fear emerges in the human psyche and reflects itself in many ways, most prominently as worry. Studies show that there are only two kinds of situations over which we generally worry: (a) the inevitable, and (b) the remediable. The former worry is unavoidable, even irresistible, and we can do nothing about it. Therefore, we need not worry over the inevitable, just keep smiling. The remediable can be remedied through self-effort and right actions. Naturally then, why should we waste time and energy worrying? Let us roll up our sleeves and work to remedy the situation that is threatening to worry us. In all charity and kindness, we should not allow worry to always worry us. Why not take the battle into the enemy's land, and worry the worry that comes to worry us ? Worry not. No dynamic individual should waste his or her precious time in this suicidal mood of unintelligent worry.

All we need is a little more self-confidence and faith in the Great Protector, the Lord of the Universe. Surrendering to Him mentally in love and dedication let us throw ourselves into action. Who will waste time in worrying except the dull or the inept? No intelligent person need do it. Let us overcome all our self-polluting worries. Remember we are walking the spiritual path.

And yet, to worry over little things has become almost a fashion. An optimistic young person dashing cheerfully in and out of activities is looked down upon in our society today as an irresponsible, carefree youngster. We seem to value the person who is weighed down with imaginary fears, weeps at possible difficulties, shudders at probable troubles, or goes mad with the memories of the worries. Society looks at such a person as being respectable and responsible. But alas! It is always such people who soon fall ill, and we hear of a sudden death — a case of thrombosis!

Worry is such a wasteful and extravagant habit of the mind. It costs much and produces poor results. Let us not waste our time and energy in ruinous worry. That vitality, which is dissipated by worrying, if directly turned to positive action, can remove all possible chances of worrying in the future. Honestly, this is so logical that it is almost obvious — and yet, we keep on worrying over the very question why we worry about our phantom, fiendish worries. ... "Stop worrying" is the only effective remedy for all worries.

Worry is not in itself a sin, but like all sins it is precious energy misspent in unproductive and wrong directions. Correct thinking has helped many patients with their worries. Not only were they able to cure themselves but they also came to discover a happy contentment in the new lifestyle of dynamic and creative activity. By making a habit of reading and reflecting upon scriptures, such as the Upanishads and the *Bhagavad Gītā*, the mind is enchantingly and easily turned into the vista of "right thinking." This is proven in the autobiographies of great men who reveal to us the secret of their stupendous achievements. The quickening power of a scriptural saying has often revolutionized man's life and character.

The Art of Relaxation

In our present life, we carry with us an unnecessary load of worries, fears, anxieties, and excitements. Yet others say they are a necessary part of the price we have to pay in our present-day life for all its vaster wealth, larger trade, greater production, and world-wide contacts. However, we need not allow that load to crush us; in spite of them, we can learn to straighten our backs and shoulders. Vedanta advises a path — a simple but effective daily exercise of "Be quiet" the art of relaxation.

At least for ten minutes each day let us try to be totally relaxed, not only in body, but also in our mind and intellect. Allow the body to sit in total relaxation. As the body relaxes, most people find that the mind dashes forth even wilder, and our intellect, too, becomes stormy with swirling thoughts. In this pernicious tornado brought about by our own mind, we shall find all our worries and fears, regrets, passions, attachments and disappointments, a thousand petty things, totally forgotten by us, all of them splintering about and together opening up an endless column of fury and misery.

But we must have courage. We shall not despair. Calmly let us observe the mad and furious chaos. Smile, and cheerfully watch. We are not in any danger. We are just watching the wild cataclysm from the safe towers of our spiritual-strength and power-divine. Thus, maintain peace and poise in the heart, and serenely watch on.

During these moments of watching, we are but a "witness" of our own inner urges and our outer world. As a witness, a passive but alert observer, we are neither involved in them nor participating in their confusions. It is always in our involvement and participation that we become the victims of the fury within, or of the tearing storms in the outer world of problems.

This is the attitude of detachment, when the mind rests in its own poise while watching the hectic dance of happenings around and within us. Under such a situation, the mad dance of the mind becomes quiet by itself, and we sink into an all-embracing mood of quiet. This is the beginning of meditation.

Meditation is not easy. The roaring floods of events and thoughts can daze one's mind and it often slips and falls with the swell, shattering the peace within.

In order to keep the mind in peace, we must have a center for it to hold on to — and that is the feet of the Lord. Repetition of the mantra helps to support the mind firmly on the terrace of peace, from where it can continuously watch without its active participation or total involvement.

Thus, if for at least ten minutes every day in the morning or in the evening we can consciously attempt to rest our mind, it can be revived from all its fatigue and it can get recharged with all its irresistible potentialities. Conscious rest is the secret of revitalizing an exhausted mind. Surrender unto Him as a child, be then neither a son nor a father, a social being, or a national member. Let us detach ourselves from all such earthly relationships and attitudes. There, in those moments, we are just the "creatures" turned towards our "Creator." Worries and agitations will become quiet as though by the waving of a magic wand.

The Lord, the Supreme, dwells in the heart of all and His Glory peeps out through our equipment (body, mind, and intellect). When we tune up and thus purify our equipment, the Divine shines out with a greater dash, and we call these rays of His Glory, shooting out through us, as our abilities and efficiencies.

Among the wondrous phenomena of this universe, the human body appears to be the most unique and self-repairing machine. Give rest to the body, it will correct itself; hence naturopaths recommend long rest and fasting. There is no disease that the body cannot throw out by this direct method. Similarly, by giving "rest" to the mind-intellect equipment, it will revive itself; hence, spirituo-paths (sages) recommend long rest and meditation. There is no illness that the mind cannot shake off by this subtle process.

Great plans of action can be undertaken only by great men and women. A person is powerful according to the amount of energy, concentration, and tranquility of mind he can bring into his undertaking, together with confidence in himself and faith in the goal he has chosen to reach. This self-confidence can be generated and continuously maintained even in the face of dire difficulties only if we hold on to our convictions. Where do our convictions come from? They come from knowledge gained from studies of the scriptures, reinforced through deeper reflection, which then becomes our understanding. When we live our understanding, it crystallizes into our convictions. The dejected personality in us can be revived and refilled through intelligent living and study of scriptures, assimilating them through reflection, accepting the creative ideas, and keeping a high ideal in our mental vision. This is how we can overcome fear and worry.

XII

Gratitude Eradicates Worry
by M. J. Ryan

You cannot be grateful and unhappy at the same time.
A woman to Dr. Tom Costa

If worrying were a paying job, I would be a rich woman. Somehow during my childhood, I got the idea that worrying could actually stave off future disaster, and as I entered adulthood, I became convinced that if I were to stop worrying, took my eye off the ball, as it were, that something dreadful would happen. If I worried enough about being poor, I wouldn't be. If I worried enough about my partner's safety, nothing would happen to him. If I worried enough about my stepson's health, he wouldn't get sick. There was no room in my heart for happiness because worry took up all the space. (Indeed I was convinced that if I were too happy, it would somehow hex the situation. If I got too happy about love, for example, I wouldn't worry sufficiently and therefore it would be taken from me.)

In my forties, I have been working on letting go of my compulsive worrying, and I have been amazed at how swiftly a sense of gratefulness banishes the worrywarts. And I've tried many other things — asking myself what is the worst thing that could happen and imagining going through that to a new place; noticing without judgment my worry; indulging it; pushing it away. None of these has been as effective as tapping into a sense of appreciation *in this moment* for what I do have.

Worried about money? I focus on the fact that so far, I have always had what I needed and right now, I have enough. Worried

77

about health? I focus on the amount of good health I'm thankful to be experiencing right now. Worried about — my favorite — a loved one being taken suddenly in an accident? I focus on how grateful I am that they are in my life right now.

I think tapping into the wellspring of gratitude works for two reasons. First, worry is always about the future, if only the next hour or minute, whereas gratitude is in the here and now. Cast over your list of worries. Aren't they always about what might or might not happen? You are worried about the reaction of your boss tomorrow to your presentation. You're worried about how you are going to afford to send your son to college. You're worried about the test results. In every case, you project yourself into the future and imagine something bad happening. As André Dubus points out, "It is not hard to live through a day if you can live through a moment. What creates despair is the imagination, which pretends there is a future and insists on predicting millions of moments, thousands of days, and so drains you that you cannot live the moment at hand." Gratitude brings you back to the present moment, to all that is working perfectly right now. Tomorrow may bring difficulties, but for right now, things are pretty good.

Gratefulness also eliminates worry because it reminds us of the abundance of our universe. Yes, something bad might happen, but given all that you have received so far, chances are you will continue to be supported on your journey through life, even in ways you would never have guessed or chosen for yourself.

XIII

Overcoming the Fear of Death
by Swami Adiswarananda

The fear of death is the root of all fears. Life is being, but death is non-being. No one escapes death's cruel jaws. ... However we may want to forget death, death does not forget us. But to accept death as the end of everything makes life meaningless. "There is, then, nothing to be hoped for, nothing to be expected and nothing to be done save to await our turn to mount the scaffold and bid farewell to the colossal blunder, the much-ado-about-nothing world!"[1] The notion of enjoying life while ignoring the question of death works well when a person is young, but as he grows older he begins to hear the drumbeats of death getting louder and louder. His optimism turns into pessimism. To enjoy life by being oblivious of the reality of death is infantile and absurd. Our attempt to see only the bright side of life is futile.

Those who accept death as inevitable but still try to get compensation hereafter do not really face the question of death. Everlasting life in terms of time is irrational. That which begins in time will also end in time. Even the longest life will come to an end. The idea of physical immortality is a fanciful dream.

The True Identity of a Person

Fear of death, according to Vedanta, is rooted in our mistaken self-identity. Is a human being just a physical entity made of muscles, blood, and bone, or a mental being made of thoughts and memories? Is there anything beyond that? For physical scientists, man is nothing more than a material entity made of carbon, hydrogen, nitrogen, oxygen, sulphur, and other elements. Sociologists define man as a member of a family, group, nation, or race. Psychologists define man in terms of his thoughts and feelings. All such scientific descriptions, however, leave out an essential part of man, namely his soul — the only conscious entity, without which a human body is absolutely valueless.

The body of man is sometimes described as the city of the soul — a city of nine or eleven gates. The nine gates consist of the eyes, the ears, the nostrils, the mouth, and the organs of evacuation and generation. Two additional gates are the navel and the aperture at the top of the head. According to the seers of the Vedas, a human being has three bodies, one inside the other. First is the gross physical body. It is material by nature and is produced by a combination of the gross elements. It consists of bone, flesh, blood, and other substances. Depending upon food for its existence, it endures as long as it can assimilate nourishment. Nonexistent before birth and after death, it lasts only for a short interval between birth and death. The second body is the mind with its thoughts and memories, and the third body is made of I-consciousness. A human being uses his gross body in the wakeful state, his subtle mental body in the dream state, and his third body in dreamless sleep. The ignorant identify themselves completely with the body. The book-learned consider themselves a combination of the body, the mind, and the self. But the seers realize that the soul, or self, is distinct from the body and mind. This self, which is the focus of the deathless Universal Self, is our true identity.

Death Is Never the End

Death is disintegration of the physical body and is never the end of the story. When the physical body becomes broken due to illness, old age, or accident, the soul, along with the other two bodies, leaves the gross body and looks for another gross body to inhabit. The consciousness of the three bodies is consciousness borrowed from the soul. Deep identification with the body is the cause of the fear of death. The body, being material, is time-bound, and subject to six changes — birth, subsistence, growth, maturity, decline, and death — that are common to all material entities. Being identified with the body, a person follows the destiny of the body. When the body dies he thinks he is dying. But this is not so. The deathless soul only *appears* to die when the body dies.

The Vedic seers speak of the soul's rebirth. This rebirth is governed by the law of karma that says that our thoughts, actions, and desires determine our destiny. The *Bhagavad Gītā* describes death as one of the series of changes: "Even as the embodied Self passes, in this body, through the stages of childhood, youth, and old age, so does it pass into another body. Calm souls are not bewildered by this."[2] Rebirth gives the soul an opportunity to make things better in the next life. The very fact that life is ever changing indicates that there is some entity within us that is changeless. This changeless entity is our true Self, the constant witness to the changing phenomena of life. There is no escape from the cycles of birth and death until the Self is discovered. ...

The Soul's Journey to Freedom

The soul's three basic desires — immortality, unrestricted awareness, and unbounded joy — are attained only when it discovers its true identity, the all-embracing Self. In search of its identity, the soul changes bodies and places, and finally, knowing the limitations of all pleasures and realizing that everything finite is shadowed by death, it practices detachment and desirelessness and realizes its immortal Self. Immortality is the return of the prodigal son to his all-loving father. It is the return of the reflection of the sun to the sun. It is the river of individual consciousness meeting the infinite ocean of Pure Consciousness. It is the realization that we are like leaves of a tree and that our true identity is the tree. It is our separative existence joining the infinite existence of absolute freedom. So the Upanishad says:

"There is one Supreme Ruler, the inmost Self of all beings, who makes His one form manifold. Eternal happiness belongs to the wise, who perceive Him within themselves — not to others."[3]

The journey to this final freedom is a solitary one — alone a person is born, alone he suffers, and alone he dies. By realizing his true Self he becomes united with all beings and things and attains to final freedom. Only then comes the end of all sorrow, all fear, all anxiety.

The doctrine of rebirth is the most plausible theory to help us understand the meaning of life and the diversities of existence. Each person is born with a blueprint of his or her mind that carries the impressions of past lives. Death seems fearful because we died many, many times before. Although we do not remember the incidents, the effects of those experiences remain stored in the conscious mind in a minute form. Shri Krishna tells Arjuna (*Bhagavad Gītā*), "Many a birth have I passed through, O Arjuna, and so have you. I know them all, but you know them not, O Scorcher of Foes."[4] In the Bible, Jesus identifies John the Baptist as the prophet Elias reborn. "If ye will receive it, this is Elias, which was for to come."[5]

The Exhortations of Vedanta

Death is an inescapable and inevitable reality. To ignore it is utter foolishness. To avoid it is impossible. To hope for physical immortality is absurd. Vedanta exhorts in this regard as follows:

(a) *Make death a part of life by understanding that life without death is incomplete. As soon as we are born, we begin to die.* Life is sacred and so we cannot afford to squander it in daydreams, fantasies, and false hopes. Life without death, pleasure without pain, light without darkness, and good without evil, are never possible. We must either accept both or rise above both, by overcoming embodiment through the Knowledge of the Self. Death is certain for all who are born. As the *Bhagavad Gītā* says: "For to that which is born, death is certain, and to that which is dead, birth is certain. Therefore you should not grieve over the unavoidable."[6]

(b) *Develop immunity against death by practicing meditation and dispassion.* In meditation we try to reach our true identity, the deathless Self, by crossing over the three states of consciousness — waking, dream, and deep sleep — and becoming *videha*, or bereft of body-consciousness. In this practice, we partially and temporarily die in our physical and mental existence. Along with meditation, practice dispassion, which is knowing that nothing material will accompany us when we leave this earth, and that nothing in this world can be of any help to us to overcome death.

(c) *Build your own raft.* Vedanta compares this world to an ocean, the near shore of which we know, while the far shore remains a mystery to us. The ocean has bottomless depth, high winds, fearful currents, and countless whirlpools. Life is a journey, an attempt to cross this ocean of the world and reach the other shore, which is immortality. No one can take us across this ocean. Vedanta urges us to build our own raft by practicing meditation on our true Self. No practice of this self-awareness is ever lost. As we go on with our practice, all our experiences of self-awareness join together and form a raft of consciousness, which the Upanishads call the "raft of *Brahman*." Sitting on this raft of *Brahman*, a mortal crosses the ocean of mortality: "The wise man should hold his body steady, with the three [upper] parts erect, turn his senses, with the help of the mind, toward the heart, and by means of the raft of *Brahman* cross the fearful torrents of the world."[7]

The word *Brahman* in the verse signifies Om. Repetition of the word and meditation on its meaning are prescribed for this practice. Vedanta asserts that Self-Knowledge, or Knowledge of *Brahman*, alone can rob death of its paralyzing fear. So long as this Self is not cognized and realized, life will be shadowed by death and the world we live in will be the world of sorrow and suffering.

(d) *Free yourself from all attachments.* Our attachments and desires keep us tied to our physical existence. We often hope for the impossible and want to achieve the unachievable. To free ourselves from these attachments and desires, we need to cleanse ourselves. Just as we cleanse our body with soap and water, so do we cleanse our mind with self-awareness. The *Mahābhārata* advises us to bathe in the river of *Ātman*: The river of *Ātman* is filled with the water of self-control; truth is its current, righteous conduct its banks, and compassion its waves. O son of Pandu, bathe in its sacred water; ordinary water does not purify the inmost soul."[8]

(e) *Know your true friends.* Know that our only true friends are our good deeds — deeds by which we help others in most selfless ways. At death, everything of this world is left behind; only the memories of all the deeds we performed in this life accompany us. The memories of good deeds assure our higher destiny and give us freedom from fear of death, while the memories of bad deeds take our soul downward. Therefore, a person must try to accumulate as many memories of good deeds as possible while living.

(f) *Perform your duties.* Life is interdependent. For our existence and survival, we are indebted to God, to our fellow human beings, and to the animal and vegetable worlds. Many have to suffer to keep us happy, and many have to die for our continued existence. We are indebted to all of them. To recognize this indebtedness and make active efforts to repay them is the sacred duty of life. By doing our duties, we become free from all sense of guilt. Be a blessing to all, not a burden. Remember, when you were born you cried, but everybody else rejoiced. Live your life in such a way that when you die everybody will cry, but you alone will rejoice.

(g) *Know for certain that death has no power to annihilate your soul.* Our soul, our true identity, is the source of all consciousness. It is separate and different from our body and mind, which are material by nature and are subject to change and dissolution. The consciousness of the soul in each of us is part of the all-pervading Universal Consciousness and is the deathless witness to the changes of the body and mind. The Universal Consciousness is like an infinite ocean and we are like drops of water. We rise to the sky from the ocean, and again we fall into the ocean as raindrops. All will in the end, sooner or later, come together as part of the ocean. In the words of Swami Vivekananda:

> One day a drop of water fell into the vast ocean. When it found itself there, it began to weep and complain just as you are doing. The great ocean laughed at the drop of water. "Why do you weep?" it asked. "I do not understand. When you join me, you join all your brothers and sisters, the other drops of water of which I am made. You become the ocean itself. If you wish to leave me, you have only to rise up on a sunbeam into the clouds. From there you can descend again, a little drop of water, a blessing and a benediction to the thirsty earth."[9]

Footnotes:

[1] W. Macneile Dixon, *The Human Situation,* (Gifford lectures *1936-37*), as quoted in *Man in Search of Immortality,* by Swami Nikhilananda, Ramakrishna-Vivekananda Center, New York, 1994, p. 26.

[2] Swami Nikhilananda, trans., *The Bhagavad Gītā,* 2:13, (New York: Ramakrishna-Vivekananda Centre, 1992), 72.

[3] *The Upanishads,* Volume I (*Kaṭha Upaniṣad,* 2:2.12), p. 175.

[4] *The Bhagavad Gītā* (4:5), p. 124.

[5] *Matthew,* 11.14.

[6] *The Bhagavad Gītā* (2:27), p. 79.

[7] *The Upanishads,* Volume II (*Śvetāśvatara Upaniṣad,* 2:8), p. 91.

[8] As quoted in *Self-Knowledge (Ātmabodha),* trans. Swami Nikhilananda, Ramakrishna-Vivekananda Centre, New York, 1989, p. 172.

[9] His Eastern and Western Admirers, *Reminiscences of Swami Vivekananda,* Advaita Ashrama, 1964, pp. 265-66.

XIV

Is This an Act of Faith or an Act of Fear?

by Debbie Ford

Every important choice we make is being guided by one of two places: either it is an act of faith or it is an act of fear. Faith opens the door to a new future. It allows us to take new routes and explore different avenues. When we are grounded in faith, we have the courage to travel to destinations we've never visited. This extremely potent question — "Is this an act of faith or is it an act of fear?" — supports us in making choices from our highest selves, from the part of us that is deeply connected to all that is and all that will be. When we are making choices that are sourced by our spiritual essence and are grounded in faith, we experience unbounded freedom.

Faith is a friend by our side. When we allow it in, faith acts as the floor beneath our feet. When we make choices rooted in faith, we trust that there is a power, an unseen force, guiding us. When we have faith, we know that we are being taken care of. Faith gives us the ability to look beyond our immediate circumstances and imagine brave new choices for the future. Faith means trusting in something beyond what we know. Having faith that we are part of a bigger whole allows us to melt away our separateness. Faith gives us strength and reassurance and leaves us bathed in the wisdom that we are never alone.

Faith is the foundation for a spiritual life. When we make the choice to act from faith rather than fear, we are able to view the world from a higher perspective. Faith invites us to believe in something we cannot see, feel, or know. When our actions are based on faith, we are choosing to put our trust in something besides our fears.

Fear, on the other hand, keeps us rooted in the past. Fear of the unknown, fear of abandonment, fear of rejection, fear of not having enough, fear of not being enough, fear of the future — all these fears and more keep us trapped, repeating the same old patterns and making the same choices over and over again. Fear prevents us from moving outside the comfort — or even the familiar discomfort — of what we know. It's nearly impossible to achieve our highest vision for our lives as long as we are being guided by our fears.

Our fears tell us what we can and cannot do. They tell us to play small and be safe. Our fears cause us to try desperately to hold on to habits and behaviors even when they no longer serve us. The root of all our repetitive negative patterns is fear. Fear keeps us going around and around in circles, never allowing us to envision an exit from lives that bind and defeat us.

What are we afraid of? We are afraid that life won't bring us what we want or think we need. We fear that if we try and fail, it will hurt too much. Or maybe we're afraid that if we do succeed we'll feel guilty and won't be able to handle it. We fear that if we stand up and claim our piece of the world, we will be rejected or abandoned by our friends and families. We fear that our lives will become unmanageable and we will lose control. Any time we do something that is inconsistent with our past — that is different from who we've been or who we think ourselves to be — we are confronted with our fears.

Yet if we continue to make choices from a place of fear, we will miss vital opportunities and guarantee ourselves a future that is no more than a continuation of our past. If we are really honest with ourselves, we will see that many of our actions and choices arise out of the fear that losing what we already have — even if we don't like it — will be worse than not getting what we want. Our fear drives us to take a job we don't want because we're afraid we won't have enough money. Our fear

DEBBIE FORD

may keep us in a dead-end relationship because we're scared we won't find anyone else, or it may lead us to make choices that dishonor ourselves because we're afraid another opportunity won't come our way. When fear is in control of our choices, we are left with few options. Fear fuels self-doubt and internal criticism. Fear destroys dreams and exterminates possibilities. Fear shuts us down, while faith opens us up. Our fears are made up of our anger, pain, worries, resentments, and insecurities; faith is made up of hope, possibility, trust, and an inner belief in the benevolence of the universe... .

Living a Faith-Based Life

We have to ask ourselves, "Where is my faith right now? Is my faith in my fears? Am I placing my faith in the idea that I'm not going to get what I want? Or am I placing my faith in the perfection of the universe? Do I have faith that I will be guided to the circumstances that will give me exactly what I need?"

Most of us misplace our faith. We have more faith in our pain, our past, and our negative beliefs than we do in our innate right to be happy. We have faith in being a victim; we have faith that we are going to come up short or get cheated or that life won't work out for us. We don't trust that our needs will be met. We don't trust that we'll have everything we want. When we place our faith in our fears, we remain closed and shut off from the very things we desire the most. When we have faith in our negative beliefs, in our flaws, and in our insecurities, we rob ourselves of the opportunity to grow and change and blossom into the divine beings that we were meant to be. Asking ourselves this question will immediately expose how much or how little we trust the world.

When we choose to live a faith-based life, our first task is to resign as general manager of the universe. Faith asks us to surrender control of our lives. Surrender is an act of courage. It is a divine path that gives us access to realities beyond what we know. To surrender and live a faith-based life is to acknowledge the divine nature of the universe. To surrender affirms that we trust in a higher power to tend to our needs and guide us in the direction of our heart's desires. Surrender is an act of faith; it's a gift that you give yourself. It's saying, "Even though I feel scared or I'm not sure where I am going, I trust that all will turn out in my highest and best interest." Faith equals trust. Faith offers us hope and opportunity and promise. If we choose to live in faith, we will be blessed with the support and the partnership of the universe.

PART THREE

You Can: You Will

What can we fear?
What should we fear?
We possess something within us that is living and vibrant,
but if we are closed to that Divine influence it cannot
make any impression on us.
As we grow conscious of this Higher Power, we throw
away our littleness.
We feel exalted and uplifted.

Swami Paramananda

A perfect sage who is established in non-duality is the most courageous of men. The courage of a soldier on the battlefield, or of a thief is only inert courage. It is not real courage at all. It is only brutal ferocity born of hatred and jealousy. The pure and untainted courage born of wisdom of the Self alone is real courage. Let there be no dualism in the mind. Always think of cosmic love and universal brotherhood

When there is love and brotherhood, there is no enmity, no superiority or inferiority. Of course, this is an intermediate stage. The final stage is the feeling of the oneness of all. All is *Brahman*. All merge in *Brahman*. There is *Brahman* alone throughout the universe.

Swami Sivananda

XV

Freedom from Fear
by Aung San Suu Kyi

[*The following was first released for publication to commemo-
rate the European Parliament's award to Aung San Suu Kyi of
the 1990 Sakharov Prize for Freedom of Thought. The award
ceremony took place in her absence at Strasbourg on 10 July
1991. Aung San Suu Kyi is the daughter of Bogyoke Aung San.
He was a national hero and revolutionary of Burma who was
assassinated on July 19, 1947.*]

It is not power that corrupts but fear. Fear of losing power corrupts those who wield it and fear of the scourge of power corrupts those who are subject to it. Most Burmese are familiar
with the four *a-gati,* the four kinds of corruption. *Chanda-gati,*
corruption induced by desire, is deviation from the right path in
pursuit of bribes or for the sake of those one loves. *Dosa-gati* is
taking the wrong path to spite those against whom one bears ill
will, and *moga-gati* is aberration due to ignorance. But perhaps
the worst of the four is *bhaya-gati,* for not only does *bhaya,* fear,
stifle and slowly destroy all sense of right and wrong, it so often
lies at the root of the other three kinds of corruption.

Just as *chanda-gati,* when not the result of sheer avarice, can
be caused by fear of want or fear of losing the goodwill of those
one loves, so fear of being surpassed, humiliated or injured in
some way can provide the impetus for ill will. And it would be
difficult to dispel ignorance unless there is freedom to pursue
the truth unfettered by fear. With so close a relationship between

fear and corruption it is little wonder that in any society where fear is rife corruption in all forms becomes deeply entrenched.

Public dissatisfaction with economic hardships has been seen as the chief cause of the movement for democracy in Burma, sparked off by the student demonstrations in 1988. It is true that years of incoherent policies, inept official measures, burgeoning inflation and falling real income had turned the country into economic shambles. But it was more than the difficulties of eking out a barely acceptable standard of living that had eroded the patience of a traditionally good-natured, quiescent people — it was also the humiliation of a way of life disfigured by corruption and fear. The students were protesting not just against the death of their comrades but against the denial of their right to life by a totalitarian regime, which deprived the present of meaningfulness and held out no hope for the future. And because the students' protests articulated the frustrations of the people at large, the demonstrations quickly grew into a nationwide movement. Some of its keenest supporters were businessmen who had developed the skills and the contacts necessary not only to survive but to prosper within the system. But their affluence offered them no genuine sense of security or fulfillment, and they could not but see that if they and their fellow citizens, regardless of economic status, were to achieve a worthwhile existence, an accountable administration was at least a necessary if not a sufficient condition. The people of Burma had wearied of a precarious state of passive apprehension where they were "as water in the cupped hands" of the powers that be.

> Emerald cool we may be
> As water in cupped hands
> But oh that we might be
> As splinters of glass
> In cupped hands.

Glass splinters, the smallest with its sharp, glinting power to defend itself against hands that try to crush, could be seen as a vivid symbol of the spark of courage that is an essential attribute of those who would free themselves from the grip of oppression. Bogyoke Aung San regarded himself as a revolutionary and searched tirelessly for answers to the problems that beset Burma during her times of trial. He exhorted the people to develop courage: "Don't just depend on the courage and intrepidity of others. Each and every one of you must make sacrifices to become a hero possessed of courage and intrepidity. Then only shall we all be able to enjoy true freedom."

The effort necessary to remain uncorrupted in an environment where fear is an integral part of everyday existence is not immediately apparent to those fortunate enough to live in states governed by the rule of law. Just laws do not merely prevent corruption by meting out impartial punishment to offenders. They also help to create a society in which people can fulfill the basic requirements necessary for the preservation of human dignity without recourse to corrupt practices. Where there are no such laws, the burden of upholding the principles of justice and common decency falls on the ordinary people. It is the cumulative effect on their sustained effort and steady endurance which will change a nation where reason and conscience are warped by fear into one where legal rules exist to promote man's desire for harmony and justice while restraining the less desirable destructive traits in his nature.

In an age when immense technological advances have created lethal weapons which could be, and are, used by the powerful and the unprincipled to dominate the weak and the helpless, there is a compelling need for a closer relationship between politics and ethics at both the national and international levels. The Universal Declaration of Human Rights of the United Nations proclaims that "every individual and every organ of society" should strive to promote the basic rights and freedoms to which all human beings regardless of race, nationality, or religion are entitled. But as long as there are governments whose authority is founded on coercion rather than on the mandate of the people, and interest groups which place short-term profits above long-term peace and prosperity, concerted international action to protect and promote human rights will remain at best a partially realized struggle. There will continue to be arenas of struggle where victims of oppression have to draw on their own inner resources to defend their inalienable rights as members of the human family.

Revolution of the Spirit

The quintessential revolution is that of the spirit, born of an intellectual conviction of the need for change in those mental attitudes and values which shape the course of a nation's development. A revolution, which aims merely at changing official policies and institutions with a view to an improvement in material conditions, has little chance of genuine success. Without a revolution of the spirit, the forces which produced the iniquities of the old order would continue to be operative, posing a constant threat to the process of reform and regeneration. It is not enough merely to call for freedom, democracy, and human rights. There has to be a united determination to persevere in the struggle, to make sacrifices in the name of enduring truths, to resist the corrupting influences of desire, ill will, ignorance and fear.

Saints, it has been said, are the sinners who go on trying. So free men are the oppressed who go on trying and who in the process make themselves fit to bear the responsibilities and to uphold the disciplines which will maintain a free society. Among the basic freedoms to which men aspire that their lives might be full and uncramped, freedom from fear stands out as both a means and an end. A people, who would build a nation in which strong, democratic institutions are firmly established as a guarantee against state-induced power, must first learn to liberate their own minds from apathy and fear.

Always one to practice what he preached, Aung San himself constantly demonstrated courage — not just the physical sort but the kind that enabled him to speak the truth, to stand by his word, to accept criticism, to admit his faults, to correct his mistakes, to respect the opposition, to parley with the enemy, and to let people be the judge of his worthiness as a leader. It is for such moral courage that he will always be loved and respected in Burma — not merely as a warrior hero but as the inspiration and conscience of the nation. The words used by Jawaharlal Nehru to describe Mahatma Gandhi could well be applied to Aung San: "The essence of his teaching was fearlessness and truth, and action allied to these, always keeping the welfare of the masses in view."

Gandhi, that great apostle of nonviolence, and Aung San, the founder of a national army, were very different personalities, but as there is an inevitable sameness about the challenges of authoritarian rule anywhere at any time, so there is a similarity in the intrinsic qualities of those who rise up to meet the challenge. Nehru, who considered the instillation of courage in the people of India one of Gandhi's greatest achievements, was a political modernist, but as he assessed the needs for a twentieth-century movement for independence, he found himself looking back to the philosophy of ancient India: "The greatest gift for an individual or a nation ... was *abhaya*, fearlessness, not merely bodily courage but absence of fear from the mind."

Fearlessness may be a gift but perhaps more precious is the courage acquired through endeavor, courage that comes from cultivating the habit of refusing to let fear dictate one's actions, courage that could be described as "grace under pressure" — grace which is renewed repeatedly in the face of harsh, unremitting pressure.

Within a system that denies the existence of basic human rights, fear tends to be the order of the day. Fear of imprisonment, fear of torture, fear of death, fear of losing friends, family, property or means of livelihood, fear of poverty, fear of isolation, fear of failure. A most insidious form of fear is that which masquerades as common sense or even wisdom, condemning as foolish, reckless, insignificant, or futile the small, daily acts of courage which help to preserve man's self-respect and inherent human dignity. It is not easy for a people conditioned by fear under the iron rule of the principle that might is right to free themselves from the enervating miasma of fear. Yet even under the most crushing state machinery courage rises up again and again, for fear is not the natural state of civilized man.

The wellspring of courage and endurance in the face of unbridled power is generally a firm belief in the sanctity of ethical principles combined with a historical sense that despite all setbacks the condition of man is set on an ultimate course for both spiritual and material advancement. It is his capacity for self-improvement and self-redemption that most distinguishes man from the mere brute. At the root of human responsibility is the concept of perfection, the urge to achieve it, the intelligence to find a path towards it, and the will to follow that path if not to the end at least the distance needed to rise above individual limitations and environmental impediments. It is man's vision of a world fit for rational, civilized humanity which leads him to dare and to suffer to build societies free from want and fear. Concepts such as truth, justice and compassion cannot be dismissed as trite when these are often the only bulwarks which stand against ruthless power.

XVI

Triumph Over Fear
by Swami Sivananda

Freedom from fear can be achieved by liberation from the objects of fear. Reeducating the mind, bringing forth the power of the spirit, dealing with practical affairs, and diligently putting into practice the knowledge that one possesses are all essential factors to overcome fear. One must feel that no object is to be feared.

In all cases, one must distinctly understand that seeing and hearing alone does not produce the sensation of fear. A child is not usually afraid of his or her parents. But when they put on a strange countenance or yell in an unnatural way, the child becomes frightened. The parent's action gets firmly rooted in the mind. Also, the child develops a hereditary weakness in later life. This memory is scarcely washed off even after reaching adulthood. So children should not be frightened.

Here fear should not be confused with startle. Schoolboys, when they see their teacher's head at the corner of a street, flee away. This does not mean fear. On the other hand, if the teacher takes a cane in his hand, the child suffers some sort of infliction and imagines impending injury. Consequently he fears his teacher.

But how do we conquer fear? Whenever a child is afraid of something, we first tell him that there is nothing to be feared thus denying the object of fear. Denial is the first step in the procedure. Subsequently we explain to the child the actual thing, the truth. We thus convince him that it was only his fancy that created the sensation in him. We positively affirm and assert what is true. Similarly, even as we grow, we must develop constantly the knowledge that there is nothing in the universe to cause fear. The subconscious mind, which is first startled by an unusual sight or incoherent voice, should be assured that all such things are false, and must become well acquainted with the knowledge of the Truth behind everything. When fear is completely removed, nothing can hurt us.

People in well-lit cities and urban areas are afraid to move in darkness. They imagine something untoward will happen causing pain, injury, or discomfort. At the same time, many sages and renunciates roam about in the dark hills and live in caves.

Mere reeducating the mind will not strengthen courage. Putting the knowledge into practice on every occasion is quite essential. At many Vedantic lectures we find speakers advocating that what men are afraid of as snakes are really only ropes, but because of their untrained minds the listeners fail to see this and thus do not gain any strength from the lecture. Thus well-developed knowledge coupled with practice can relieve us from fear.

Developing Love and Devotion

You should not have any dualism in mind. You must always develop cosmic love and universal brotherhood. When there is love and brotherhood, there is no enmity. There is no superiority of power. There is no pleasure or pain. Ultimately there is no fear. This is a preliminary stage. The final stage is the feeling of oneness of all. All are *Brahman*. There is *Brahman* alone pervading throughout the universe. There is no second thing in His creation at all. This knowledge entirely uproots fear and brings one into eternal peace. Fear does not emanate from one's own Self. This is the secret. Knowledge of *Brahman*, the eternal Truth, totally annihilates fear.

The Truth is to be pronounced and meditated upon. Recitation of Upanishads, *Śruti*, Vedas, and hymns produces vibrations. These vibrations remove all inflections. Many incurable diseases, causing fear of death in the minds of the sufferers, are cured by these vibrations alone. The lives of saints and sages are full of stories where their faith protected them from disease and fear.

Drowning waves of fear may at times rush down upon us. We may lose mental balance for a while. We may be oversensitive and agitated. Memories of the past may haunt us; our imagination soars and we picture disaster after disaster awaiting us. Yet, under all these circumstances, we must put complete faith in God, take refuge in Him, and fully believe that He alone can deliver us.

Overcoming in this way will not suffice. This must be brought into practice. We must first face only that of which we are afraid. For example, to overcome stage fright, being on stage in front of an audience is the only way to cure it. Running away will not help. If one is afraid of the dark, one must face darkness and understand that the object, which caused the fear, is nothing but something that one has to deal with on a daily basis.

Many undergo drastic, alarming abnormality in sleep, sometimes worse than in waking. This is all due to loading the mind with stray thoughts while retiring. One should never go to bed in a state of worry or fear, nor with a heavy heart, nor brood over what is going to happen. Before retiring, everyone must eradicate all such thoughts and meditate upon God. We must have perfect peace in mind and soul. If one is unable to meditate upon God, let them loudly recite some hymn or poem peaceful, and deep sleep is guaranteed.

If we meditate upon statements of Truth, our inner eye of wisdom opens, we receive the gift of right understanding, and we know the Truth. This is worship of God. This is adoration to the Lord and it liberates us from bondage.

While working mentally and practicing physically at all times, dwelling upon divine thoughts and remaining in a higher stratum of mind, we not only overcome fear but merge in *Brahman*.

"Whence all speech turn back with the mind without reaching; he who knows the bliss of *Brahman* fears not at any time — is not afraid of anything." *Brahmānanda Valli* (4:9)

Methods to Eradicate Fear

1. *Victory over Fear.* As you think, so you become. As you think, so you develop. As is your ideal, so gradually your life will become. This is so, because there is a great transforming power in thought.

Take then the life of perfect men like Bhishma from *Mahābhārata* and think of their deeds and their life and ideals. Your life will be filled with purity and courage and you will become a noble, perfect person. The thought will transform you into its own likeness. Man becomes what he worships, and becomes what he thinks. This is indeed true.

Sit with closed eyes in the early morning. Meditate on courage, the opposite of fear, for half an hour. Think of the advantages of courage and the disadvantages of fear. Practice the virtue during the day. Feel that you actually possess courage to an enormous degree. Manifest it in your daily life. In some weeks or months fear will be replaced by courage. Repeat the formula "Om courage" mentally, several times daily.

Meditate and assert: "I am all courage. I am an embodiment of courage. I am like Bhishma. I am a great hero. My will is very powerful. I am not afraid of anything. I am bold and chivalrous. Courage is my birthright. OM OM OM."

It is very difficult to attack fear directly. Fear is very strong. You have been a victim of this negative trait in hundreds of lives. It has taken deep root. Put the seeds of courage in your heart. Allow it to grow. Fear will die by itself. The positive always overcomes the negative. This is an immutable psychological law. This is the *Pratipakṣa-Bhāvanā* — method of *Rāja Yogīn*. Try this method again and again. You are bound to succeed.

May you attain triumph over fear by cultivating courage through the *Pratipakṣa-Bhāvanā* method, or the method of thinking on the opposite!

2. *Feeling the Presence of God.* God is all-pervading. He is always with you. He is in you, around you. He is not far to seek. He cannot be perceived through the physical eye. Your sense of

touch cannot help you. He has to be realized through the inner eye of wisdom.

Modern civilization has enslaved people to such an extent that they are incapable of any original expression, thought, or deed. They do not care to think of their routine actions — how their activities progress, what they are running after, or what goal they are marching towards. Inventions, innovations, and contrivances have eased men from their labor and human skill. The conservation of energy in this direction has only created laziness in them. More sensual desires and perceptions have begun to sway them. Lost in the ever-pouring luxuries of life, the true mission is once and for all forgotten. People do not think wherefrom their daily requirements come, who the unfailing and non-stopping supplier is, where His abode rests, how to have His vision, what to request of Him, and how to revere Him. No amount of study and research in physical geography, vegetable kingdom, various industrial technologies, physiology, and other sciences will solve these problems nor even give a clue to the solution. This scientific knowledge is subject to various hypotheses, axioms and data, which by themselves are under controversies. This knowledge will in no way aid one to arrive at the source. The source is really beyond all these conceptions. Its abode cannot be located by running the finger over a colored map. The Dweller and His abode can be seen only through the inner eye and right understanding. Concentration, meditation, and sublime thoughts are the pathways to this abode.

Most people are unable to keep their minds upon God or meditate upon divine thoughts. This is all due to want of training. Realization is always through practice. Practice comes out of proper training. Proper training requires consultation of learned men. This is "Initiation in the right path."

In all ages you meet with such great personalities who are always ready to help but may not advertise themselves as such. It is left to you to find such men, to choose your own Guru, to obey him implicitly, to serve him with all sincerity and earnestness, and to express your thirst for knowledge.

Vain discussions and intentional test-questions must be strictly avoided. You must be regular in your practice.

There are again persons who say that they are unable to meet even a single person of such qualities for their Guru. Though it is firmly held that no perfection can be attained in any line without a Guru, it may well be asserted that God is near and dear to you, as He is to everybody. Sincere and earnest attempt will have its own fruits. It is not on this plea that concentration and meditation have to be cast off.

Because a man does not understand the language of a film, does he refrain from watching films? He avails himself of every opportunity to accompany his friend who is able to interpret and who is already in the groove. Even if he is unable to get it, he pushes himself anyway and tries his best to decipher the whole film racking his brain. He makes earnest efforts to improve his knowledge in this line by purchasing synopsis, bulletins, and magazines. He is restless until he acquires some knowledge. At no stage does he stop and put an end to this quest of knowledge. In due course every actor or actress lives at the tip of his tongue. He becomes profusely enlightened in this art. He speaks hours and hours about the talents of various film stars. What is all this due to? Is he not training himself earnestly, honestly, sincerely, and virtuously in this particular line? Did he wait for a Guru? What a pity it is that a man indulges so much in trivial things discarding the vital mission of life?

It is quite common for people to complain that when they begin to contemplate upon God, their mind wanders here and there and their thoughts become engaged with mundane affairs. This is again due to lack of training and want of definite willpower. True. It is very difficult, in fact, extremely difficult to fix the mind at first instance upon God. An entirely different, superior, and higher stratum of mind is needed for this practice. This has to be developed well.

The mind is full of lust. It is always restless. It traverses through all spheres — good or bad. It has to be wound up by the triple cord of devotion, concentration, and meditation. It must always be kept under control.

Try to be alone for a few minutes every day. If you cannot afford this, utilize every scrap of leisure you presume to enjoy. Select a lonely place, a riverbank, the top of a mount, the open terrace of your house, seashore, a simple pleasant meadow, a corner in a temple, church or mosque, or a private room. Purge all your wavering thoughts. This will be quite easy in any of the above localities as all the senses will be drawn by the exquisite, beauty of the spot or landscape or by the deep silence pervading all around. If necessary, burn incense or scented sticks, which will always keep you alert.

There are two distinctive ways for worship of God. One, the "All-pervading Nature" and the other, "Here and here alone." If one is to sit down and contemplate on the omnipresence of God, that is, presence in the sun, in the moon, in the stars, in anything and everything he comes across, perhaps he might become lost in immensity. On the other hand one may localize the presence of God at the initial stage, which he may develop later into the former method.

Having steadied the mind either by gazing at a particular spot, or the picture of any form of God or Guru or tuning the ears to the murmur of the river or receding waves of the sea, utter slowly in a low tone the statement "God is Now Here" or "God is in This Room." First repeat "God is Now Here" in a deep meditative way. Then relax for a while and again repeat. Do this untiringly till you are immersed in your statement. Now you realize the presence of God.

Do not stop with this. This is not the ultimate aim. Existence Absolute, Knowledge Absolute, and Bliss Absolute (*Sat, cit, ānanda*) is the supreme aim. After experiencing "God is Now Here," repeat "His Presence Fills Me From Head to Foot." By repeated utterances, realize His existence in you. In the same way practice "His Presence is Joy," "His Presence is Love," and "His Presence is Peace." Whenever your mind attempts to wander, repeat these statements loudly until it comes around. Morning hours are most suitable. This practice will free you from fear and fill you with courage, joy, and peace.

If this is practiced untiringly, a sense of supreme joy, cosmic love, and eternal peace will reign over you. What to speak of the radiance of such a realized Yogi? How glorious will he shine in the world.

May all know this easy way for the realization of God! May all practice this with definiteness and self-will. May all share His blessings. May the all-merciful Lord help them and relieve them from the struggle of *saṁsāra*.

3. *Devotion to God Eradicates All Fears*. God bestows perfect security on His devotees and removes all sorts of fears. He transforms the sense of insecurity and fear into one of confidence and faith. He saves them from panic and despair.

Mira was tormented by her husband in a variety of ways, but Lord Krishna protected her and removed all her fears. The cup of poison was changed into nectar. Cobra was changed into *Śāligrāma* and a garland of flowers. She was shut in a cage where there was a hungry tiger. The tiger did not eat her but kissed the feet of Mira. This was all due to the grace of Lord Krishna.

Lord Hari removed all the fears of Prahlada. Prahlada was tormented by his cruel father. Prahlada was thrown into the sea. He was trampled under the feet of an elephant. He was rolled down from the top of a hill. He was thrown into the fire. But he was saved by Lord Hari. Lord Vishnu removed all his fears.

A devotee sees only the Lord in all names and forms. He beholds Lord Hari everywhere. How can there be fear, then, for him?

Take refuge in the Lord, in His name and grace. All fears will vanish completely. He will bestow strength, fortitude, courage, presence of mind, and so on in you.

Abandon desires *rāga-dveṣa* and all sorts of worldly attachment. Pray and meditate: "Lord Hari! I am Thine. O Lord Hari! All is Thine. Thy will be done. Fill my heart with courage. Shower Thy grace on me. Let my mind be attached to Thy lotus feet. Let me feel Thy presence, everywhere. Let me behold Thee in all forms. Reveal Thy form to me. Guide me, protect me.

XVII

The Address of Happiness
by Thich Nhat Hanh

If you want to know where God, the Buddhas and all the great beings live, I can tell you. Here is their address: in the here and now. It has everything you need, including the zip code.

If you can breathe in and out and walk in the spirit of "I have arrived, I am home, in the here, in the now," then you will notice that you are becoming more solid and more free immediately. You have established yourself in the present moment, at your true address. Nothing can push you to run anymore, or make you so afraid. You are free from worrying about the past. You are not stuck, thinking about what has not happened yet and what you cannot control. You are free from guilt concerning the past and you are free from your worries about the future.

Only a free person can be a happy person. The amount of happiness that you have depends on the amount of freedom that you have in your heart. Freedom here is not political freedom. Freedom here is freedom from regret, freedom from fear, from anxiety and sorrow. "I have arrived, I am home, in the here, in the now."

"I am solid, I am free." This is what you feel, what you become, when you arrive in the here and now. You're not just telling yourself this—you will see it; you will feel it. And when you do, you will be at peace. You will experience *nirvāṇa*, or the kingdom of God, or whatever you may like to call it. Even if you are not caught by a lot of worries, if you are not solid and free, how can you be happy? To cultivate solidity and freedom in the present moment is the greatest gift we can give ourselves.

Dwelling in the Ultimate

"In the ultimate I dwell." The ultimate is the foundation of our being, the ground of being. The ultimate, or God, or the divine, is not separate from us. We are in it all the time. It is not somewhere up there beyond the sky. But we have to live in our true home in order to dwell in the ultimate, in order to live in the ultimate.

It is like the wave and water. If we look into a wave, we see that a wave can have a beginning and an end. A wave can be high or low. A wave can be like other waves, or it can be different. But the wave is always made of water. Water is the foundation of the wave. A wave is a wave, but it is also water. The wave may have a beginning and an end, it may be big or small, but with water there is no beginning, no end, no up, no down, no this, no that. When the wave realizes and understands this, it is free from the fear of beginning and end, up and down, big and small, this and that.

In the historical dimension, we have time and space, and pairs of opposites: right and wrong, young and old, coming and going, pure and impure. We look forward to beginning and we are afraid of ending. But the ultimate dimension does not have any of these things. There is no beginning or end, no before or after. The ultimate is the ground that makes the historical dimension possible. It is the original, continuing source of being. It is *nirvāṇa*. It is the kingdom of God.

Our foundation is *nirvāṇa*, the ultimate reality. You can call it God or the kingdom of God. This is the water in which we live. You are a wave, but at the same time you are also water. You have a historical dimension and you also have an ultimate dimension. If we understand that our true nature is of no birth, no death, no coming, no going, then our fear will depart and our pain and suffering will vanish.

A wave does not have to die in order to become water. She is water right here and now. We also do not have to die in order to enter the kingdom of God. The kingdom of God is our very foundation here and now. Our deepest practice is to see and touch the ultimate dimension in ourselves every day, the reality of no birth and no death. Only this practice can remove our fear and suffering entirely. Rather than saying, "In the ultimate I dwell," you may like to say, "In the kingdom of God I dwell," or "In the Buddha land I dwell."

Releasing Sorrow

Suppose someone was able to transport you by jet to the kingdom of God or the Pure Land of the Buddha. When you arrived, how would you walk? In such a beautiful place, would you walk under pressure, running and anxious like we do so much of the time? Or would you enjoy every moment of being in paradise? In the kingdom of God, or the Pure Land, people are free and they enjoy every moment. So they do not walk like we do.

The Pure Land is not somewhere else; it is right here, in the present. It is in every cell of our bodies. When we run away from the present, we destroy the kingdom of God. But if we know how to free ourselves from our habit energy of running, then we will have peace and freedom and we will all walk like a Buddha in paradise.

What we carry with us determines in which dimension we dwell. If you carry a lot of sorrow, fear and craving with you, then wherever you go you will always touch the world of suffering and hell. If you carry with you compassion, understanding and freedom, then wherever you go you will touch the ultimate dimension, the kingdom of God.

Wherever the practitioner goes, she knows she is touching the kingdom of God under her feet. There is not one day when I do not walk in the kingdom of God. Because I practice freedom and compassion wherever I go, my feet touch the kingdom of God, the ultimate dimension everywhere. If we cultivate this kind of touching, then the important elements of solidity and freedom will be available to us twenty-four hours every day.

"I have arrived, I am home." The home of the wave is water. It's right there. She does not have to travel thousands of miles in order to arrive at her true home. It's so simple and so powerful. I would like to invite you to memorize this little poem and to practice and remember it many times a day. In this way you will touch the ultimate dimension and always remember your true home.

XVIII

What if God Blinks?
by Rachel Naomi Remen

When I was small, God was still discussed in the public schools. I remember one assembly in which our principal, a fundamentalist, delivered a fire-and-brimstone kind of sermon to the entire grammar school. She read a passage from the Bible to us and told us it was important that we kneel and pray three times a day because we needed to remind God that we were there. Thinking back, she may not have said this in so many words, but this is what I took away. You prayed because you had to make Him look at you. If God turned His face from you, she told the hushed assembly of children, you would wither up and die, like an autumn leaf. And this part I am sure of, she actually held up a large dried and withered leaf. Even as a five-year-old it seemed to me that God had a lot of other things on His mind besides me. And in between the times that I was praying, He might blink and then what would become of me? I remember the fear, the enormous terror. *What if God blinks?* I became so obsessed with this question, so fearful, I was unable to sleep.

My parents were young socialists who considered religion to be "the opiate of the masses," and my grandfather, who was a rabbi, was my only connection to a reality larger than social well-being and the class struggle. When I was this small, I actually thought of God as a friend of his, like the men who came over to smoke cigars and play gin rummy in our kitchen with my father.

As these fears were not something I could discuss with my parents, I had to wait until my grandfather visited. It was probably only a few days, but I remember the waiting. I don't think you can feel such anguish and aloneness as an adult. You have to be very young.

When I finally got my grandfather to myself I told him what had happened. Shaking, I asked him the fearful question: "What if God blinks?" and at last my terror overwhelmed me and I leaned against his shoulder and began to cry. My grandfather stroked my hair to comfort me. Despite his gentleness he seemed distressed and even angry.

But in his usual calm way, he answered my question with some questions of his own. "Nashume-le," he said (and by the way, for years I thought that my grandfather's name for me meant "Little Naomi" — it actually means "Little Soul"), "if you woke up in the night in your room, would you know if your mother and father had gone out and left you alone in the house?" Still crying, I nodded yes. "How would you know that?" he asked. "Would you see them and look at them?" I shook my head no.

"Would you hear them?"

"No."

"Could you touch them?"

By then I had stopped crying and I remember puzzling over his questions because it seemed obvious to me that I would simply *know* that I wasn't alone in the house. I told him this and he nodded, pleased. "Good! Good! That's how God knows you're there. He doesn't need to look at you to know that you are there. He just *knows*. In just the same way you know that God is there. You just *know* that He is there and you're not alone in the house."

God's presence in the house is an inner experience that never changes. It's a relationship that's there all the time, even when we're not paying attention to it. Perhaps the Infinite holds us to Itself in the same way the earth does. Like gravity, if it ever stopped we would know it instantly. But it never does.

This inner knowing is a way in which I orient myself, an unfailing point of reference. Its effect on my life is as profound, as deep as gravity's influence on my body. More than anything else, my sense of not being alone in the house has been what has allowed me to accompany people as they meet with pain, illness, and sometimes death.

XIX

The State of Fearlesness
by Swami Chinmayananda

> When this *Ātman* attains the fearless oneness with *Brahman* who is invisible, incorporeal, inexplicable and unsupported, then he becomes free from fear. When, however, this makes any slightest distinction in *Brahman*, then there is danger for him. That very same *Brahman* Himself becomes the source of fear for him who makes a difference, and reflects not.
> *Taittirīya Upaniṣad* (2:7.3)

An individual who comes to experience his oneness with *Brahman* becomes free from fear. Fear can come only from something other than oneself. No one is afraid of himself. When a seeker successfully realizes his oneness with the entire Universe, the sense of distinction ends and thereafter he has no occasion to feel the sense of fear at anything.

To convey this idea that fearlessness can come only at the realization of the individual's oneness with the Truth, the *Upaniṣad* gives the negative statement also. *Brahman* Itself becomes a source of fear for him who makes even the slightest distinction in it. The moment we recognize an objective God other than ourselves reveling in heaven and we do not seek our oneness with Him, agitations and fears come to storm our hearts and minds. Perfect tranquility and peace come only when we establish our unquestioned oneness with Truth. Perfect happiness is only in the fulfillment of love. Love is fulfilled only when the lover and the beloved merge to become one single mass of love experience. Similarly, when the ego-center in us loses all its separative Consciousness and comes to experience its unbroken and definite oneness with the *Ātman* it comes to live the infinite state of perfection and fearlessness in Itself.

The same Truth which gives fearlessness to the realized provides occasions for fear to those who do not give enough meditative thought to the discriminative analysis of the Unreal and the Real. The ego is "*Ātman* playing the fool amidst the unreal." To awaken itself to the Real is to rediscover Its Divine omnipotent nature and in this Self-discovery is the State of Fearlessness. Those who do not make the necessary discriminative analysis of the Real and the unreal, of the true and the false, in their delusory identifications come to feel themselves different from the Real and their realization is never complete.

The Supremacy of Spirit over Matter

> Out of His fear the wind blows. Out of fear the Sun rises.
> Out of His fear runs fire, as also Indra, and Death, the fifth.
> *Taittirīya Upaniṣad* 2:8.1.

In the phenomenal world, in spite of its confusing plurality and endless multiplicity of things, there seems to be some golden chord of uniformity inasmuch as this external jigsaw puzzle follows strictly a definite law in its moment-to-moment existence and activity. There is certainly a concord that runs through the noisy discord of the world. There is a silent rhythm seen imperceptibly running through the endless variety of confusing movements. Seasons similarly follow one after another rhythmically. Each object in the universe strictly conforms itself to its own nature. There are the natural laws that strictly follow all scientific observations. The sun is never dark; the moon is never hot; fire is never cold! A cow begets no lion; a tigress begets no bird. The innumerable laws of instincts and emotions observed among the vegetables, animals, and human lives are all strictly pursued everywhere in nature.

A law is always promulgated by a lawgiver; and wherever we find strict adherence to the law, it is always because of the fear for the lawgiver. Similarly, if in nature we find that the natural laws are irrevocably declared and strictly followed, certainly, we have to assume that behind the phenomenon of nature there is a definite lawgiver who strictly executes the law. He, ever standing, as it were, just behind Nature with a raised whip threatening them with total annihilation at the simplest disobedience.

This idea is brought out by the *śruti* in order to establish the Supremacy of the Spirit over matter, and also its dynamism in it. Also this declaration conclusively proves that this spirit is not a nonexistent nonentity, but an existent Reality which can be courted and experienced, as full of Bliss, omnipotence and omniscience.

Five main observations are made here by the *śruti*: such as the movement of air, the rising of the sun, the heat of the fire, the light of the moon, and, fifthly, the very principle of decay and death that sustains the perishable nature of a finite world, called Death. All of them indicate that the entire phenomenal world is not a haphazard idle dream of a mad man, but it is an intelligent scheme ordered by a Dynamic Divine Power which executes Its will very strictly and fully through Its established laws of behavior and reaction. This is a Vedic hymn quoted here in support of the previous mantra, which declared that he who rediscovers the spiritual center becomes fearless, because he thereby becomes the very Truth, whose dictatorial sovereignty is the irrevocable sanction behind Nature's laws.

XX

Peace

by Andrew Stirling

[*The following is from a sermon preached by the Rev. Dr. Andrew Stirling on January 30, 2005 in Toronto.*]

Francis Bacon, the British philosopher, once said: "It is miserable to have a state of mind when you have few desires, but many fears." Bacon is suggesting that fear is indeed a very real force in human existence. It is so powerful that it can alter one's whole perception of life, so that one does not enjoy desires and pleasures when they come along; the fears that come at night and prevent us from sleeping; the fears that dominate our attitudes towards others and to the world; the fears that can permeate the very depths of our souls. It is a miserable state of mind to have that many fears, and therefore, few really good desires.

This became very evident to me last Sunday. As you know, I was privileged to preach at Yorkminster Park Baptist Church as part of the Churches-on-the-Hill pulpit exchange. It was an exceedingly cold and bitter morning. I arrived early to preach to that congregation, but my throat was dry, and my body and my hands were cold, and since I had a few minutes, I decided to walk down Yonge Street and pop into a coffee shop for a hot cup of coffee to nestle towards my chest for a few minutes. I went in and ordered my double-double, and of course a little doughnut on the side, and in no time I was warmed up with a glow that went from the bottom of my toes to the top of my head. I felt ready.

As I walked out, I could see a man huddled with his back towards one of the newspaper stands. He had a blanket wrapped around himself and a rather dark cap on and a scarf tied tightly around his neck, as he sat on the ground looking lonesome and cold. I asked him if he would like a cup of coffee, and he said he would love one. So, I asked him what he took. I went in, got it, brought it out, and gave it to him, but then I thought, "You know, this man really should not be in this state." I said to him "On a cold morning like this (it was -30°C), you should be in a shelter. Is there anything that I can do or someone that I can call right now to help you find a place where you can go?"

A look of utter fear came across his face. He said, "No, Father, please don't do that! I don't want to go to a shelter!"

I said, "Fine, we won't do that, but why not? It is so cold and this is so dangerous, and I am worried for you."

He told me his reason, as if to unburden himself about the state of his life. He said, "Actually, I am a recovering alcoholic, and I think I have beaten it. I think I have done it, thanks to AA. I am grateful I am no longer an alcoholic."

I said, "That's wonderful! I am very glad for you. May God be praised!"

Then he said, "But there's another problem: I also have an addiction to gambling, and that is why I am in the state I am now. A lot of gambling goes on underground in the shelters. In some of them, you gamble for the best beds or the best food or the next packet of cigarettes, or the next drink or a little extra protection. I don't think most people realize that this goes on, not in all, but in some of the shelters. I dare not for one minute go to a place where I might get caught up in gambling, for I would probably lose even the clothes that I have right now."

It was obvious from the look on his face that even though I persisted in saying, "Still you should," that he wouldn't go.

He stopped me in my tracks and said, "There's no 'still' about it, I cannot go." The fear in his eyes was so strong and so powerful that it caused him to sit on the ground on Yonge Street in -30°C temperatures.

Fear, my friends, will make us do incredible things. John Berryman, who in 1964 won the Pulitzer Prize for his brilliant book, *Dream Song,* had to wrestle with many demons in his life. One of them was alcoholism. In his battle with alcoholism, he finally succumbed to the depression that sometimes comes with it.

One day, he flung himself off a bridge over the Mississippi and died. Before he did, he wrote something fascinating: "We must travel in the direction of our fears." Now, I have wondered what Berryman meant. If he meant that we should confront our fears, to use a quote from David MacLennan, written in a sermon he preached here many years ago, he said there was a need to exteriorize our fears. In other words, to not repress them, but to name them, to speak them and to let them be known.

Then, I would say we should walk in the direction of our fears. We should not run away from them. But, if it should mean that those fears dominate us, that we allow those fears to set the agenda or the path of our lives, then clearly to Berryman I would say "No!"

In today's reading from the Gospel of St. John, Jesus is dealing with fear and with peace. He is dealing with the fears of his disciples as he looks into their eyes at the time before his departure, before his crucifixion. He looks them in the eyes and he can tell that they are stressed and they are worried and they are frightened, for they have no idea what life will be like without him, so much so that they ask him questions like, "Where are you going?" and "Can we go with you?" and "Where is the way?"

They want to go with Jesus, but he is talking about leaving, and so in the midst of their fears, in the midst of their confusion, in the midst of their sense of everything coming to a head after having followed him for three years, Jesus says, "My peace I leave with you, not as the world gives, give I unto you, let not your hearts be troubled." With the promise of the Holy Spirit, Jesus believes he has given the disciples everything that they need to face the days and the weeks that will follow.

So I asked myself, "What did those words mean to Jesus' disciples then, and what do they mean for us now?" When Jesus said, "My peace I leave with you," can you and I grasp that same peace even in the midst of our own fears, and can we share that peace with those who experience fear in their own lives? The answer, of course, is "Yes," but what did Jesus really mean?

Clearly, he meant something unique. He said, "My peace I leave with you." Not a peace alongside a group of other therapies; not a peace of a temporary respite from the stresses of life. This is not a peace that just gives you a balm for your soul once in a while. Jesus is not offering a spa or a health club membership to get you through the cold days of winter. He is giving something greater: he says, "My peace I leave with you."

However, when you look at the word peace, you can see that there is even greater depth and meaning. I know sometimes we preachers quote Greek as if it somehow drips off the back of a box of cereal in the morning, a common word used here and there. But sometimes there is a meaning to a Greek word that really does capture the nuance of what is said. It does in this case. Jesus says to them, "I leave with you my *eirene*" and the word "*eirene*" has as its equivalent in Hebrew the word "*shalom*." It is the same word. I leave with you *shalom*; I leave with you *eirene*; I leave with you my peace. *Shalom* and *eirene* mean an actual state of being. I am leaving you a state of being, and it is a state of being that is different from another Greek word, "*polemos*," from which we get the word "polemic," a time of disturbance, a state of conflict, or a state of aggravation.

A New State of Being

In other words, Jesus is not just offering them a temporary respite from the trouble of the world, he is offering them a new state of being. He is saying to these disciples that he will leave this for them, in such a way that only he can give it, because what he is going to do is bear the cross. What he is going to do is rise from the dead through the power of the Father, and through that very gift of his death and resurrection they are going to have a new state of being in which to live: a new way of existing, so if hardships come, they will be reconciled with God and with one another, through what Jesus is doing. "My peace I leave with you."

It is unique, but it is also, as you can see as the text continues, universal. It is a universal peace. Jesus not only says "My peace I leave with you," but he also promises to send them the comforter, and that through the power of the Father, this comforter will be left with the disciples. The power of the Holy Spirit, in other words, will continue to give them this peace.

Now, for those of us who do not have Jesus around to sit with us in our time of sorrow, who do not have him physically right there next to us to hold our hand and to comfort us when we have fears, we now have the power of the same Spirit, and as Jesus said to the disciples, this Spirit will remind us of everything that he has said. "You will recall what I have done by the very power and gift of this Spirit." As believers today, we have exactly that same source of strength: the Spirit is the presence of the living Christ with us now. We are not left comfortless. Our hearts need not be troubled. The new state of being is life lived through and by the very power of that comforter, the Holy Spirit. When we face our travails, and when we face our challenges, and we look eye to eye with our fears, the Spirit of that living Christ is with us.

Sometimes, my friends, our fears do control the way that we live our lives. Sometimes we really do need the power of that Spirit to help us through. John Broder, one of my favorite writers in the *New York Times,* wrote an article a few years ago about a problem that teenagers were having in the 1980s. They were taking bags and spraying an aerosol into it, which they would sniff to get high. The manufacturers of this aerosol product were terrified of liability suits, because these young people could die if they inhaled too much of their product. The chemical in the aerosol that produced the high was called 1-1-1 trichloroethane. The manufacturers wanted to stop people from sniffing trichloroethane, so they put on warnings on the cans that it can kill you, but it made no difference; teenagers still sniffed it. Eventually, the manufacturers hired a lawyer from Washington, DC to advise them as to what kind of language they could put on the can to stop teenagers from sniffing it.

They suggested they put bigger warnings, citing even greater dangers, but the lawyer said, "No, you don't understand teenagers. If you tell them that it is more dangerous, they will assume there is more of the drug in it and that they will be able to get higher; you'll only make it more attractive." Instead, he advised them to appeal to what teenagers fear the most. So they came out with a warning label that said, "This product may cause your hair to fall out and your face to be disfigured." Well, I think we are all vain, and the younger we are, the vainer we are. Strange as it sounds, teenagers are more afraid of being ugly than of dying. Now, this warning wasn't strictly true: Your hair does not fall out if you sniff trichloroethane, and you will not have an ugly face, but I suppose once you are dead your hair does fall out and your face doesn't look great, so it is true in the end. At any rate, the warning worked, and teenagers all around the world stopped sniffing trichloroethane for fear of being disfigured and losing their hair.

Sometimes you need to address the fears that control your life, and it is the Spirit of God that enables us to confront them in a meaningful way. Some time ago, I met a woman who was faced with a very difficult decision. She had been diagnosed with cancer, and it was so bad that if she was to defeat the cancer, she would require an operation that would disfigure her for life. It was the most horrible situation. She said, "I am really struggling with this, Andrew. I don't know what to do. All I would ask is for you to pray for me throughout this ordeal until I decide what to do."

It was a no-win situation. I covenanted with her to pray for her from then until she made the decision. Just before it was time for her to go to the doctor, she phoned me and said, "I just want to let you know that I have decided to have the operation." She continued, "You know why? A great peace has come upon me. I have realized that when I get to Heaven, God will not look at me in my disfigurement, for the disfigurement will have gone.

He will only look at me and wonder whether I loved and cared for my family; whether I embraced the life he gave me; whether I lived my life for Him." Such is the power of the spirit. Even when facing the most terrible fears and the most awful decisions in life, the power of the Spirit transforms those fears in a way that is beyond our understanding.

Sometimes, my friends, our fears come from within, and sometimes our fears come from without, from other people and other situations. As I watched the ceremony marking the 60th anniversary of the liberation of Auschwitz last week, there was a moment at the beginning, when the trains came along the tracks and the wheels were squeaking. The camera panned over those who were in attendance, and you could tell that some of them had been there 60 years ago, had heard the brakes on the wheels on those tracks before, from the fear you could see in their eyes. It was just like the man I saw on the street last Sunday: fear of the other, fear of the world, fear of life. Those fears are powerful things. The only force that can help overcome them in a meaningful and substantial way is the new state of being, the peace, the *eirene* that Jesus brings: the power of the Spirit.

XXI

The Free Ticket
by Kanchan Mukherjee

Come holidays and there is a mad rush for tickets to go to holiday resorts. For many it is time for a break from the stressful routine life. Scenic spots and hill stations are the favorite destinations. People don't mind sweating in the crazy scramble for tickets, having anxious moments in confirming hotel reservations and travel bookings and some even lose sleep in this process. On the other hand, although within reach, rarely does one pick the free ticket offered, a ticket for the inner journey.

This ticket requires no money, no waiting or sweating in serpentine queues, no anxious moments. This ticket is provided by God and enables one to embark on our journey within our own Self. It is an extremely joyous journey, requiring no more than a sitting space in a quiet corner of one's own room.

When we travel on our external journey we usually reach our destination quite tired and so seek rest. On the contrary, on reaching the destination of our internal journey we are relieved of tiredness and become ready for a much meaningful time ahead. This is because we have experienced inner bliss, our true nature. This unique experience of inner bliss has the effect of removing our anxieties, worries, and tensions. It is a free ticket to a priceless treasure offered by none other than the creator himself.

Much time, energy, and money is spent on traveling outside in the hope of getting that alluring peace of mind. But the best we get is the temporary pleasure of running away from our daily activities and hoping the pleasure would last forever. Having spent large sums of money, staying in the "best" hotels, and visiting the "best" places, when we feel "satisfied," it is like settling for a map rather than for the territory. Once back from the external journey, we all succumb to the same old tensions, anxieties and stress which we had left behind.

However the returns of our internal voyage are non-diminishing in nature. They are like credit points accumulated with each journey. The more you travel the more you accumulate and that is why it is worth all the trouble, as it is associated with spiritual credit that we gain. A person blessed with this inner experience would repeatedly take this free ticket, for he knows, the returns for accepting this gift of God has no parallels. This gift is available *only* to the human form of life and before it becomes too late let us pick this free gift.

We are indeed privileged to have examples of great souls like Shri Ramakrishna, Gautama Buddha, Swami Vivekananda and others, who have experienced this bliss and shown us the path to Self-realization. We must respond to the invitation and reap rich fruits of this luminous experience. Look at the spiritual opulence these divine lives manifested and gauge for yourself what awaits you.

XXII

The Peace of Surrender
by Swami Tejomayananda

Surrender is the language of devotion. In the language of Knowledge that same state is called as Self-realization. It is a state of total annihilation of the ego. In the path of knowledge (*jñāna yoga*), the focus is initially on making the mind subtler through inquiry (*vicāra*), and finally the ego (the "finite I" notion) is destroyed by the knowledge of one being the infinite Self. In the path of devotion (*bhakti yoga*), the first step itself is surrendering of the ego at the altar of the Lord. All efforts thereafter are put forth in this direction alone.

There are many aspects of surrender. Normally when we say that we have surrendered, we do not really know what it means. The attitude, "Thy will be done, not mine," shows surrender. When Mirabai, the great saint was sent poison by her husband, she drank it with joy, because she truly believed the Lord sent it. The poison turned into nectar. Such is the glory of total surrender.

Surrender and self-will cannot co-exist. On the one hand, we say that we have surrendered to God, and on the other we hold on to our own will and ego. Sometimes we attribute things to God's will, and sometimes to our own. A criminal justifying his action as God's will has to accept the judge's decision also as God's will. Either we exercise our own will, and own up to the results in a gracious manner, or we surrender totally to His will. We cannot have it both ways. We may say that we have surrendered our will, we have handed over all our responsibilities to the Lord, and that He will take care of everything, but are we truly convinced that the Lord will do all of it? We pray to God, but at the same time we harbor doubts whether He will listen and take care of us. Only when we trust God fully are we able to experience the benefit of total surrender.

Why Surrender and to Whom?

Why do we seek refuge? When it rains suddenly, we run for shelter. In the scorching heat of the sun, we seek the shade of a tree. When we are suffering from a disease, we seek the help of a doctor. In a financial crisis, we look for support from a rich colleague. In family troubles, we seek the company of a sympathetic friend. We seek the support, help, company, or refuge of another to alleviate our physical and mental sorrows and for solutions to life's problems.

We naturally surrender to one who is capable of alleviating our sorrow. However much a pauper sympathizes with our condition; we do not turn to him for help in time of a financial crisis. We cannot surrender to one who is insecure or miserable himself! Such a person may only add to our own insecurity and sorrow, or in turn seek sympathy and help from us. Also, we find that the person who may be able to give us financial help may not be able to provide psychological solace or physical security. So, it is best to surrender to the Lord alone, as in Him we get support, help, and solace for all our problems at once. We can attain real peace in the Lord alone, for He is omniscient, omnipotent, all bliss, ever present, and all love. Tulsidasji says, "Surrendering unto Him, I have found supreme peace."

The Lord's Assurance

On the battlefield of Kurukshetra, when Arjuna was confused about the right course of action, Lord Krishna gave him the knowledge of the *Bhagavad Gītā*. After expounding various means to purify the mind and gain knowledge through *karma yoga* (the path of action), *dhyāna yoga* (the path of meditation), and so forth, the Lord concludes with the famous *Bhagavad Gītā* verse (18:66): "Give up all other means/duties/paths and surrender all unto Me alone. I shall free you from all sins. Rest assured, do not grieve." Also, in the *Vālmīki Rāmāyaṇa* Lord Rama says: "It is my vow (promise) that if a person comes to Me and says even once, 'O Lord, I am yours,' I will make him or her fearless."

Lord Krishna says again, "I will liberate him from all sins," and Lord Rama says, "I will release him from all fears." Are these promises and results different? No, sin causes fear, and fear causes sin. Both sin and fear cause bondage and sorrow. So the Lord is assuring us that those who surrender to Him will be free from all sorrow and bondage.

The Six-fold Factors of Surrender

The *Vaiṣṇava sampradāya* describes the six-fold factors of surrender:

1. Entertain favorable thoughts
2. Renounce unfavorable thoughts
3. Have firm faith that God will protect
4. Seek refuge in the Lord
5. Submit completely to the Lord's mercy
6. Express total helplessness

1. Entertain favorable thoughts. The beginning of any concept is a thought, and actions follow the thoughts. In order to surrender, all thoughts must be diverted to the Lord, "I want the Lord, I want to reach Him. I am willing to do anything that is conducive to my reaching Him. I will make myself fit for receiving His grace. I will equip my mind with the qualities that are required for gaining His vision (*darśana*). I will attend *satsaṅga*, follow the instructions of my guru, and do regular spiritual practices. I will try to please the Lord with my actions. I will serve Him in every way." To entertain such thoughts is the first aspect of surrender (*ānukūlyasya saṁkalpaḥ*).

2. Renounce unfavorable thoughts. While favorable thoughts help us rise toward the goal, unfavorable thoughts pull us down. In order to attain the Lord, we must be willing to give up anything that stands in the way. We effortlessly give up all pleasures, name, fame, power, relationships, and wealth if they prove to be obstacles in our path. We give up all objects and attachments (*viṣayatyāga* and *saṅgatyāga)* that obstructs our spiritual progress. We give up all worldly talk of pleasure, wealth, heretics, and enemies, and the company of pleasure-loving or evil-minded people. We willingly give up false notions and prejudices, and work tirelessly to renounce anger, jealousy, pride, hypocrisy, and so forth. Such thoughts and actions are called renouncing the unfavorable (*pratikūlyasya varjanam).*

3. Have firm faith that God will protect. We must have firm and doubtless faith, not only in the existence of God, but in His protection of us at all times under every circumstance. He is not only our "wish-fulfiller," but our "well-wisher." He, therefore, does what is best for us. We may not understand or appreciate His ways, but we know that whatever happens, happens for the best, as His protective and guiding hand is behind all that we get in life. He is kind and compassionate, and His love for us is unconditional. We are His children, and He will never abandon us whatever we do. No problem is too big for Him. He will take care of us; we do not have to worry. We are protected by His blessings, which He abundantly showers on us, in spite of what or who we are.

4. Seek refuge in the Lord. We may have faith, but when we actually seek refuge, it is called *goptṛtva-varaṇam.* We actually pray for protection, blessings, and grace. We ask to be liberated: "I come to you as I am; make me what You want me to be. I have come this far, take me further. Hold me. Guide me to the Truth. You have guided me till now, help me further, bless me always. ..."

5. Submit completely to the Lord's mercy. Submission means falling at the feet of the Lord in total surrender to Him. "I am Yours to do with what You wish. I have no will or wish of my own. I am like a flute in Your hands. You can play whatever tune You wish to play." With total surrender we let go of our reservations and resistance to His will. King Bali not only gave his entire kingdom to Lord Vamana but finally gave himself as well to the Lord. He surrendered all his possessions (my-ness) and his ego (I-ness). This is *atma-nikṣepa,* also called *atma-nivedanam* in the nine-fold aspects of Devotion (*nava-vidhā-bhakti*) propounded by Sage Narada.

6. Express total helplessness. As long as we think we can do things by our own effort, independent of the Lord, He does not interfere. The Lord is very democratic. He says, "If you think you can do something, go ahead and do it." As soon as we seek refuge and surrender and reveal our helplessness, He responds and comes forward to uplift us.

When we speak sweet words of helplessness and surrender, we immediately invoke His compassion and grace. The Lord is the embodiment of purity, so each thought as it objectifies the Lord, becomes pure and beautiful. The world cannot prove distracting to such a devotee, and his mind never gets tired of thinking of the Lord.

About Authors

Benson, Herbert

Herbert Benson, M.D., is the founding president of the Mind/ Body Medical Institute (M/BMI), and the Mind/Body Medical Institute Associate Professor of Medicine, Harvard Medical School. A graduate of Wesleyan University and the Harvard Medical School, Dr. Benson is the author or co-author of more than 175 scientific publications and 11 books. Dr. Benson is a pioneer in mind/body medicine, one of the first Western physicians to bring spirituality and healing into medicine.

Caponigro, Andy

Trained as a classical jazz guitarist, Andy Caponigro performed with various musical groups and taught at the esteemed Berklee School of Music in Boston. After working with many musicians and singers to help them overcome stage fright and better control their breathing for improved performances, he decided to explore breath-work in more detail. These studies led him to begin a healing practice. He works privately with people suffering from chronic illness and psychological problems who were not helped by conventional therapies, with amazing results. He continues to lead workshops and train others to use his techniques. Andy Caponigro lives in Hadley, Massachusetts.

Dozier, Rush W. Jr.

Rush W. Dozier, Jr., is a Harvard-educated, Pulitzer Prize-nominated writer and scholar, specializing in science and technology. He lives in Pasadena, California.

Fischer, Kathleen

Kathleen Fischer, Ph.D., MSW, has been a teacher, therapist, and spiritual director in Seattle for more than twenty-five years. She is the author of numerous articles and books, including the award-winning *Women at the Well, Autumn Gospel*, and *Transforming Fire*. Her most recent book is *The Courage the Heart Desires: Spiritual Strength in Difficult Times.*

Ford, Debbie

Debbie Ford is an internationally recognized expert in the field of personal transformation whose books have been translated into twenty-two languages and used as teaching tools in universities, other institutions of learning and enlightenment worldwide. Debbie earned a degree in psychology with an emphasis in consciousness studies from JFK University. In 2001 she received the Alumni of the Year Award for her outstanding contribution in the fields of psychology and spirituality. Debbie has appeared as a guest on many prominent television shows

Greenspan, Miriam

Miriam Greenspan is a renowned psychotherapist, writer, and speaker whose pioneering book, *A New Approach to Women and Therapy* helped define the field of women's psychology. It has been used as a textbook in programs of psychology, social work, counseling, and ministry in the United States, Canada, Europe, Israel, China, and Korea. Honored as a "feminist foremother" in psychology, Greenspan has given hundreds of workshops and public talks on women's psychology and therapy, and related subjects, throughout the United States and Europe.

Jeffers, Susan

Susan Jeffers, Ph.D. has helped millions of people throughout the world overcome their fears, heal their relationships, and move forward in life with confidence and love. She is the author of many books on overcoming fear. Her latest book is *The Feel the Fear Guide to Lasting Love*, which was published in the UK in May 2005 and in the US and Canada by her own publishing company, Jeffers Press, in October 2005. As well as being a best-selling author, Susan is a sought-after public speaker and has been a guest on many radio and television shows internationally. She lives with her husband, Mark Shelmerdine, in Los Angeles.

Mukherjee, Kanchan

Dr. Kanchan Mukherjee, a doctor by qualification, teaches at the Tata Institute of Social Sciences in Mumbai, India.

Remen, Rachel Naomi

Dr. Rachel Naomi Remen is one of the earliest pioneers of mind/body health. She is Clinical Professor of Family and Community Medicine at the UCSF School of Medicine and Director of the UCSF course, The Healer's Art. She is Co-founder and Medical Director of the Commonwealth Cancer Help Program featured in the Bill Moyers PBS series, *Healing and the Mind*. She is Founder and Director of the Institute for the Study of Health and Illness, a professional development program for graduate physicians who wish to develop a greater personal capacity for empathy, compassion, understanding and communication. Dr. Remen has a 45-year personal history of Crohn's disease and her work is a unique blend of the viewpoint of physician and patient. She is the author of the New York Times bestseller *Kitchen Table Wisdom: Stories That Heal*.

Ryan, Mary Jane

Mary Jane Ryan is the founder and former CEO of Conari Press, one of the most successful independent book publishing houses in the U.S. In 2000 she joined Professional Thinking Partners where she specializes in one-on-one thinking partnerships, and is one of PTP's lead workshop presenters. She is one of the facilitators of Time Out, a five-day bimonthly retreat on personal renewal for corporate executives and other professionals at Robert Redford's resort in Sundance, Utah. Mary Jane is the co-founder of the Worldwide Women's Web and editor of the award-winning book *The Fabric of the Future: Women Visionaries Illuminate the Path of Tomorrow*. A member of the International Coaching Federation and a regular columnist for *Living In Balance* and *The Works* magazines, she is a popular speaker on what she is calling the modern virtues: kindness, gratitude, generosity and simplicity.

Stirling, Andrew

The Reverend Dr. Andrew Stirling has been the Senior Minister of Timothy Eaton Memorial Church in Toronto, Ontario, Canada since July 1998. Born in the United Kingdom, he was educated in England, Bermuda and Canada. He received the Call to the Christian Ministry while living and studying in Cape Town, South Africa and in 1980 was forced to leave the country because of his opposition to Apartheid. He returned to Canada and was Ordained in the Maritime Conference of the United Church of Canada. He has been active in the academic community. In 1991 he was a Visiting Scholar at Harvard University Divinity School. He is an Instructor in Church History at the University of Toronto School of Continuing Studies. In addition, he has lectured and preached at numerous theological conferences, universities and churches throughout the world and is a member of the International Bonhoeffer Society and the Canadian Theological Society. His main areas of interest are: Trinitarian Theology, Church and State relations particularly as it relates to spiritual and social reconciliation, homiletics and the Church struggle in South Africa and Jewish Christian relations.

Suu Kyi, Aung San

For the Burmese people, Aung San Suu Kyi has become an international symbol of heroic and peaceful resistance in the face of oppression. She represents their best and perhaps sole hope that one day there will be an end to the country's military repression. As a pro-democracy campaigner and leader of the opposition National League for Democracy party (NLD), she has spent more than 10 of the past 17 years in some form of detention under Burma's military regime. In 1991 she was awarded the Nobel Peace Prize for her efforts to bring democracy to Burma. At the presentation, the Chairman of the Nobel Peace Prize Committee, Francis Sejested, called her "an outstanding example of the power of the powerless." After a period of time overseas, Aung San Suu Kyi went back to Burma in 1988.

Swami Adiswarananda

Swami Adiswarananda was born in West Bengal, India. He received his undergraduate degree and Master's degree from the University of Calcutta. Swami Vivekananda and his call to the "service of God in man" inspired him during his student days. In 1954 he joined the monastic order of Sri Ramakrishna and was ordained a monk in 1963. As a monk, he has served in various capacities in educational and cultural centers. He taught religious subjects for several years at one of the premier colleges, the Ramakrishna Mission Vidyamandira at Belur, West Bengal, India. In 1966 he was sent to the Advaita Ashrama at Mayavati in the Himalayas, where he was Joint Editor of *Prabuddha Bharata*: Awakened India, the English-language monthly journal on religion and philosophy. He served in that capacity until 1968, when he was sent to the Ramakrishna-Vivekananda Center of New York to assist Swami Nikhilananda.

Swami Chinmayananda

His Holiness Swami Chinmayananda, founder of Chinmaya Mission, taught spirituality as the art of living. Through *jñāna yoga* (the Vedantic path of spiritual knowledge), he emphasized the balance of head and heart, pointing out selfless work, study, and meditation as the cornerstones of spiritual practice. Not satisfied by worldly aspirations or his degrees in literature and law, Balakrishna Menon pursued spiritual studies for nine years in the Himalayas, under the guidance of Swami Sivananda (Divine Life Society) and the tutelage of Swami Tapovanam. He eventually came to share this Vedantic knowledge with the masses, in the form of the dynamic teacher known as Swami Chinmayananda. Swamiji is renowned worldwide as a spiritual master and one of the foremost teachers of *Bhagavad Gītā*. He is credited with the renaissance of spirituality and cultural values in India, and with the spreading of the ageless wisdom of *Advaita Vedānta*, as expounded by Adi Shankaracharya, throughout the world. Swami Chinmayananda attained *mahāsāmadhi* in August 1993. His legacy remains in the form of written, audio, and video publications; social service projects; Vedanta teachers whom he taught and inspired; and Chinmaya Mission centers worldwide, serving the spiritual and cultural needs of local communities.

Swami Ishwarananda

Swami Ishwarananda is the *ācārya* of Chinmaya Mission Los Angeles, *Kasi, Mithila,* & *Gokul*. Swamiji joined Sandeepany Sadhanalaya in Mumbai in 1991. Upon completing his *brahmacārī* training in 1993, as Brahmachari Someshwar Chaitanya, he served Chinmaya Mission Centers in Bangalore and Calcutta and eventually as resident Acharya of Chinmaya Mission Los Angeles. Swamiji was given *samnyāsa* in February of 2000. Swamiji was the Acharya in charge of Sandeepany Sadhanalaya in Mumbai for the 12th *brahmacārī* training from 2002 through 2004. Swamiji is a dynamic speaker and has given talks on Vedanta, stress management, and management techniques. Swamiji's mastery over the field of Vedanta comes through in his lucid and practical talks.

Swami Sivananda

Born in southernmost India in 1887, Swami Sivananda was a strong, athletic and active young man. Early on he demonstrated that innate passion for service and generosity that characterized his entire life. His passion for service led him to the study of medicine and, after graduation, to serve as a doctor in Malaya (now Malaysia). After about ten years he began to feel an inner call to a life of renunciation — a life dedicated to meditation, spiritual study and repetition of God's name. In 1924 he arrived in Rishikesh where he met his guru. There followed years of intense austerity and long hours of meditation as well as deep study. However, even his ardor for his spiritual practices did not prevent him from finding some time each day to offer medical help and other services to his fellow *sādhūs* and to passing pilgrims. In 1936, in order to better serve his growing family of disciples and followers, he registered The Divine Life Society Trust. A grant of land from the ruler of Tehri-Garhwal provided space for new buildings and the continuing growth of the Ashram that has continued to this day even though Swami Sivananda passed away in 1963.

Swami Swaroopananda

Swami Swaroopananda is the Director in-charge of the Chinmaya International Residential School in Coimbatore, India. This school teaches children from across the world, grooming the entire being based on the strong foundations of the Gurukula tradition of ancient India, which has been adapted to suit modern educational leverage. Earlier Swamiji was the *ācārya* (teacher and spiritual leader) of the Chinmaya Mission Australia center. In a little over a decade, Swamiji has traversed the globe several times touching the lives of thousands of eager listeners in cities as diverse as London, New York, Sydney, New Delhi, Singapore, Dubai, and Lagos. A disciple of the world-renowned Master of Vedanta, and champion of India's spiritual wisdom, Swami Chinmayananda, Swami Swaroopananda left his family's thriving business in Hong Kong at an early age to seek what he now calls, "Real answers to real problems."

Swami Tejomayananda

Swami Tejomayananda, the spiritual head of Chinmaya Mission centers worldwide since 1993, is fulfilling the vision of his guru, Swami Chinmayananda. As Mission head, Swami Tejomayananda has already conducted more than 400 *jñāna yagna* worldwide. He has served as dean or acarya of the Sandeepany Institutes of Vedanta, both in India and in California. Fluent in Hindi, Marathi and English, and lecturing and writing commentaries in all three languages he makes even the most complicated Vedantic topics clear to his audience. Swamiji excels in expounding upon a wide spectrum of Hindu scriptures, from *Rāmāyaṇa*, to *Bhagavad Gītā*, to the Upanishads. His easy manner, combined with his in-depth analyses and devotional renderings of Vedantic texts, have drawn many newcomers into the spiritual fold.

Thich Nhat Hanh

Thich Nhat Hanh was born in Central Vietnam in 1926. At the age of 16 he entered the monastic life in Vietnam, where his primary teacher was Dhyana (meditation; Zen) Master Thanh Qu Chun. Thich Nhat Hanh has combined his deep knowledge of a variety of traditional Zen teaching methods with methods from Theravada Buddhism and ideas from Western psychology to form his approach to modern Zen practice. He has become an important influence in the development of Western Buddhism. In 1956 he was named Editor-in-Chief of *Vietnamese Buddhism*, the periodical of the Unified Vietnam Buddhist Association. In the following years he founded a publishing house, the Van Hanh Buddhist University in Saigon, and the School of Youth for Social Service (SYSS), a corps of Buddhist peace-workers who went into rural areas to establish schools, build healthcare clinics, and help re-build villages.

Pronunciation of Sanskrit Letters

a	(but)	k	(skate)	t	⎰think or	ś	(shove)
ā	(father)	kh	(Kate)	th	⎱third	ṣ	(bushel)
i	(it)	g	(gate)	d	⎰this or	s	(so)
ī	(beet)	gh	(gawk)	dh	⎱there	h	(hum)
u	(suture)	ṅ	(sing)	n	(numb)	ṁ	(nasaliza-
ū	(pool)	c	(chunk)	p	(spin)		tion of
ṛ	(rig)	ch	(match)	ph	(loophole)		preceding
ṝ	(rrrig)	j	(John)	b	(bun)		vowel)
ḷ ⎰no English equivalent	jh	(jam)	bh	(rub)	ḥ	(aspira-
	ñ	(bunch)	m	(much)		tion of
	ṭ	(tell)	y	(young)		preceding
	ṭh	(time)	r	(drama)		vowel)
e	(play)	ḍ	(duck)	l	(luck)		
ai	(high)	ḍh	(dumb)	v	(wile/vile)		
o	(toe)	ṇ	(under)				
au	(cow)						

The Power of Faith
(continued on inside back page)
MANANAM BACK ISSUES
(continued from page ii)

Joy: Our True Nature
Contemplation in a World of Action
Love and Forgiveness
Saints and Mystics
Om: The Symbol of Truth
The Illusory Ego
The Source of Inspiration
The Essential Teacher
The Razor's Edge
Harmony and Beauty
The Question of Freedom
The Pursuit of Happiness
On the Path
Beyond Sorrow
Self-Discovery
The Mystery of Creation
Vedanta in Action
Solitude
The Choice is Yours

THE *Self-Discovery* SERIES

Meditation and Life
by Swami Chinmayananda

Self-Unfoldment
by Swami Chinmayananda

THE *Hindu Culture* SERIES

Hindu Culture: An Introduction
by Swami Tejomayananda

The Sanskrit word *Mananam* means reflection. The *Mananam Series* of books is dedicated to promoting the ageless wisdom of Vedanta, with an emphasis on the unity of all religions. Spiritual teachers from different traditions give us fresh, insightful answers to age-old questions so that we may apply them in a practical way to the dilemmas we all face in life. It is published by Chinmaya Mission West, which was founded by Swami Chinmayananda in 1975. Swami Chinmayananda pursued the spiritual path in the Himalayas, under the guidance of Swami Sivananda and Swami Tapovanam. He is credited with the awakening of India and the rest of the world to the ageless wisdom of Vedanta. He taught the logic of spirituality and emphasized that selfless work, study, and meditation are the cornerstones of spiritual practice. His legacy remains in the form of books, audio and video tapes, schools, social service projects, and Vedanta teachers who now serve their local communities all around the world.